Multi-Modal
Face Presentation
Attack Detection

Synthesis Lectures on Computer Vision

Editor

Gérard Medioni, *University of Southern California*
Sven Dickinson *Samsung Toronto AI Research and University of Toronto*

Synthesis Lectures on Computer Vision is edited by Gérard Medioni of the University of Southern California and Sven Dickinson of the University of Toronto. The series publishes 50- to 150 page publications on topics pertaining to computer vision and pattern recognition. The scope follows the purview of premier computer science conferences, and includes the science of scene reconstruction, event detection, video tracking, object recognition, 3D pose estimation, learning, indexing, motion estimation, and image restoration. As a scientific discipline, computer vision is concerned with the theory behind artificial systems that extract information from images. The image data can take many forms, such as video sequences, views from multiple cameras, or multi-dimensional data from a medical scanner. As a technological discipline, computer vision seeks to apply its theories and models for the construction of computer vision systems, such as those in self-driving cars/navigation systems, medical image analysis, and industrial robots.

Multi-Modal Face Presentation Attack Detection

Jun Wan, Guodong Guo, Sergio Escalera, Hugo Jair Escalante, and Stan Z. Li

ISBN: 978-3-031-00696-8   paperback
ISBN: 978-3-031-01824-4   ebook
ISBN: 978-3-031-00081-2   hardcover

DOI 10.1007/978-3-031-01824-4

A Publication in the Springer series

SYNTHESIS LECTURES ON COMPUTER VISION

Lecture #17

Series Editors: Gérard Medioni, *University of Southern California*

            Sven Dickinson *Samsung Toronto AI Research and University of Toronto*

Series ISSN

Print 2153-1056   Electronic 2153-1064

Multi-Modal Face Presentation Attack Detection

Jun Wan
Institute of Automation, Chinese Academy of Sciences,
and University of Chinese Academy of Sciences, Beijing, China

Guodong Guo
Institute of Deep Learning, Baidu Research, and
National Engineering Laboratory for Deep Learning Technology and Application, Beijing,
China

Sergio Escalera
Universitat de Barcelona and Computer Vision Center, Spain

Hugo Jair Escalante
Computer Science Department at INAOE, Puebla, Mexico,
and Computer Science Department at CINVESTAV, Zacatenco, Mexico City, Mexico

Stan Z. Li
Westlake University, Hangzhou and
Institute of Automation, Chinese Academy of Sciences, Beijing and
Macau University of Science and Technology, Macau, China

SYNTHESIS LECTURES ON COMPUTER VISION #17

ABSTRACT

For the last ten years, face biometric research has been intensively studied by the computer vision community. Face recognition systems have been used in mobile, banking, and surveillance systems. For face recognition systems, face spoofing attack detection is a crucial stage that could cause severe security issues in government sectors. Although effective methods for face presentation attack detection have been proposed so far, the problem is still unsolved due to the difficulty in the design of features and methods that can work for new spoofing attacks. In addition, existing datasets for studying the problem are relatively small which hinders the progress in this relevant domain.

In order to attract researchers to this important field and push the boundaries of the state of the art on face anti-spoofing detection, we organized the Face Spoofing Attack Workshop and Competition at CVPR 2019, an event part of the ChaLearn Looking at People Series. As part of this event, we released the largest multi-modal face anti-spoofing dataset so far, the CASIA-SURF benchmark. The workshop reunited many researchers from around the world and the challenge attracted more than 300 teams. Some of the novel methodologies proposed in the context of the challenge achieved state-of-the-art performance. In this manuscript, we provide a comprehensive review on face anti-spoofing techniques presented in this joint event and point out directions for future research on the face anti-spoofing field.

KEYWORDS

face presentation attack detection, face anti-spoofing, multi-modal data analysis

Contents

Preface

Biometric face recognition has achieved great success in the last few years, especially with the great progress in deep learning. Face recognition systems have been widely used in diverse applications, such as mobile phone unlocking, security supervision systems in railway or subway stations, and other access control systems. However, as promising as face recognition is, there also exist potential flaws that should be addressed in practice. For instance, user photos can be easily found in social networks and used to spoof face recognition systems. These face presentation attacks make authentication systems vulnerable. Therefore, face anti-spoofing technology is important to protect sensitive data, such as the user's face image and privacy in smartphones and similar devices. In this context, we organized the Chalearn Looking at People on face anti-spoofing competition, an academic challenge focusing on such important problems and relying on a new large-scale dataset created for the task, the CASIA-SURF dataset.

This book presents a comprehensive review of solutions developed by challenge participants of the face anti-spoofing challenge at CVPR 2019. The motivation behind organizing such a competition and a brief review of the state of the art are provided. The dataset associated with the challenge is introduced and the results of the challenge are analyzed. Finally, research opportunities are outlined. This book provides in a single source, a compilation that summarizes the state of the art in this critical subject, and we foresee the book becoming a reference for researchers and practitioners on face recognition.

We would like to thank all participants in the face anti-spoofing challenge at CVPR 2019, who provided us the abundant material, especially the top three winning teams. Also, we would like to thank Morgan & Claypool publishers for working with us in producing this book.

Jun Wan, Guodong Guo, Sergio Escalera, Hugo Jair Escalante, and Stan Z. Li
July 2020

Acknowledgments

This work has been partially supported by the Chinese National Natural Science Foundation Projects #61961160704, #61876179, #61872367, Science and Technology Development Fund of Macau (No. 0025/2018/A1, 0008/2019/A1, 0019/2018/ASC, 0010/2019/AFJ, 0025/2019/AKP), the Spanish project PID2019-105093GB-I00 (MINECO/FEDER, UE) and CERCA Programme/Generalitat de Catalunya, and by ICREA under the ICREA Academia programme.

Jun Wan, Guodong Guo, Sergio Escalera, Hugo Jair Escalante, and Stan Z. Li
July 2020

CHAPTER 1

Motivation and Background

1.1 INTRODUCTION

As an important branch of biometric analysis, face recognition (FR) is being increasingly used in our daily life for tasks such as phone unlocking, access authentication and control, and face-based payment [Chingovska et al., 2016, Yi et al., 2014]. Because of its wide applicability and usage, FR systems can be an attractive target for identity attacks, e.g., unauthorized people trying to get authenticated via face presentation attacks (PAs), such as a printed face photograph (print attack), displaying videos on digital devices (replay attack), or 3D masks attack. These PAs make face recognition systems vulnerable, even if they achieve near-perfect recognition performance [Bhattacharjee et al., 2018]. Therefore, face presentation attack detection (PAD), also commonly known as face anti-spoofing, is a critical step to ensure that FR systems are safe against face attacks.

1.1.1 FORMULATION OF THE PROBLEM

In order to counteract PADs, most existing approaches formulate the problem as either binary classification, one-class classification, or binary classification with auxiliary supervision.

Binary Classification. Most of research has relied on on handcrafted features (mainly texture-based ones) combined with a binary classifier distinguishing genuine vs. spoof images [Boulkenafet et al., 2017a, de Freitas Pereira et al., 2013, Komulainen et al., 2013a, Patel et al., 2016b, Yang et al., 2013]. In fact, recent methods based on deep learning adhere to this formulation, using features learned with a convolutional neural network (CNN) and a softmax layer as classifier.

One-class Classification. Because the two-class formulations are in general not robust for real-world scenarios due to the poor generalization performance in the presence of novel attack types [Fatemifar et al., 2019a, Nikisins et al., 2018], some authors [Arashloo et al., 2017, Fatemifar et al., 2019a,b] have treated the face anti-spoofing problem as one of anomaly detection, and have addressed this task with one-class classifiers. Compared to two-class classification methods, one-class classification can be robust to previously unseen and innovative attacks [Arashloo et al., 2017]. For instance, in Fatemifar et al. [2019a], the anomaly detectors used for face anti-spoofing include four types: one-class Support Vector Machine (SVM), one-class sparse representation-based classifier, one-class Mahalanobis distance, and one-class Gaussian mixture model.

Binary Classification with Auxiliary Supervision. Recently, some authors have resorted to auxiliary information for face anti-spoofing. Atoum et al. [2017] use, for the first time, facial depth maps as supervisory information, where two-stream CNNs are used to extract features from both local patches and holistic depth maps. Liu et al. [2018] propose a method by fusing features from depth maps and temporal rPPG signals. Then, Shao et al. [2019] use depth information as auxiliary supervision to learn invariant features between cross domains. These works demonstrate the effectiveness when auxiliary information are used with binary classification [Atoum et al., 2017, Liu et al., 2018, Shao et al., 2019].

1.1.2   MOTIVATION

State-of-the-art face PAD algorithms, such as those developed in the context of the IAPRA Odin project[1] [Jourabloo et al., 2018, Liu et al., 2018], have achieved high recognition rates in the intra-testing evaluation (i.e., training and testing with the same dataset). However, they generally show low performance when a cross-testing scenario is considered (i.e., training and testing data come from different datasets). Therefore, face PAD remains a challenging problem, mainly due to lack of generalization capabilities of existing methods. The latter is largely due to the fact that current face anti-spoofing databases do not have enough subjects (≤ 170), or lack enough samples ($\leq 6,000$ video clips) [Zhang et al., 2019b] compared with image classification [Deng et al., 2009] or face recognition databases [Yi et al., 2014]. This severely limits the type of methods that can be used to approach the PAD problem (e.g., deep learning models). Another missing feature in existing datasets (e.g., Chingovska et al. [2016],

---

[1]https://www.iarpa.gov/index.php/research-programs/odin

Erdogmus and Marcel [2014]) is the availability of multi-modal information. This sort of extended information may be very helpful for developing more robust anti-spoofing methods. The above-mentioned problems seriously hinder novel technology developments in the field.

A detailed comparison of the public face anti-spoofing datasets are shown in Table 1.1. Clearly, the number of subjects and samples included in most datasets is limited, also they mostly consider RGB information only. We note that the MSU-USSA dataset [Patel et al., 2016b] is not shown in Table 1.1. That is because MSU-USSA includes many objects from other existing PAD datasets, such as Idiap, CASIA-FASD, and MUS-MFSD. In order to fair comparison, we exclude MSU-USSA.

Besides, in order to study the impact that data scarcity has had in the development of PAD methods, and in general to deal with previous drawbacks, we released a large-scale multi-modal face anti-spoofing dataset, called CASIA-SURF [Zhang et al., 2019b]. The data set consists of 1,000 different subjects and 21,000 video clips with three modalities (RGB, Depth, IR). Based on this dataset, we organized the *Chalearn LAP multi-modal face anti-spoofing attack detection challenge* collocated with CVPR2019. The goal of this competition was to boost research progress on the PAD in a scenario where plenty of data and different modalities are available. Details on the challenge can be found on the challenge website.[2] More than 300 academic research and industrial institutions worldwide participated in this challenge, and ultimately 13 teams entered at the final stage.

The success of the challenge and outstanding solutions proposed by participants has motivated this compilation that aims at capturing a snapshot of the progress in face anti spoofing detection methodologies. The contributions of this volume can be summarized as follows. (1) We describe the design of the *Chalearn LAP multi-modal face anti-spoofing attack detection* challenge. (2) We organized this challenge around the CASIA-SURF dataset [Zhang et al., 2019b, 2020], proving the suitability of such resource for boosting research in the topic. (3) We report and analyze the solutions developed by participants. (4) We point out critical points on the face anti-spoofing detection task by comparing essential differences between a real face and a fake one from multiple aspects, discussing future lines of research in the field.

---

[2]Reader can apply this dataset via the link: https://sites.google.com/qq.com/face-anti-spoofing/welcome/challengecvpr2019?authuser=0.

Table 1.1: Comparison publicly available face anti-spoofing datasets (* indicates this dataset only contains images, (i.e., no video clips), ★ is short for Seek Thermal Compact PRO sensor, − indicates that this information item is not available)

Dataset	Year	Number of Subjects	Number of Videos	Camera	Model Types	Spoof Attacks
Replay-Attack Chingovska et al. [2012a]	2012	50	1,200	VIS	RGB	Print, 2 replay
CASIA-MFSD Zhang et al. [2012]	2012	50	600	VIS	RGB	Print, replay
3DMAD Erdogmus and Marcel [2014]	2013	17	255	VIS/Kinect	RGB/Depth	3D mask
I2BVSD Dhamecha et al. [2014]	2013	75	681*	VIS/Thermal	RGB/Heat	3D mask
GUC-LiFFAD Raghavendra et al. [2015]	2015	80	4,826	LFC	LFI	2 Print, replay
MSU-MFSD Wen et al. [2015]	2015	35	440	Phone/laptop	RGB	Print, 2 replay
Replay-Mobile Costa-Pazo et al. [2016]	2016	40	1,030	VIS	RGB	Print, replay
3D Mask Liu et al. [2016]	2016	12	1,008	VIS	RGB	3D mask
Msspoof Chingovska et al. [2016]	2016	21	4,704*	VIS/NIR	RGB/IR	Print
BRSU Holger et al. [2016]	2016	50+	–	VIS/AM-SWIR	RGB/4 SWIR bands	Print, 3D mask
EMSPAD Raghavendra et al. [2017]	2017	50	14,000*	SpectraCam™	7 Bands	2 Print
SMAD Manjani et al. [2017]	2017	–	130	VIS	RGB	3D mask
MLFP Agarwal et al. [2017]	2017	10	1,350	VIS/NIR/Thermal	RGB/IR/heat	2D/3D mask
Oulu-NPU Boulkenafet et al. [2017b]	2017	55	5,940	VIS	RGB	2 Print, 2 replay
SiW Liu et al. [2018]	2018	165	4,620	VIS	RGB	2 Print, 4 replay
SiW-M Liu et al. [2019b]	2019	493	1,630	VIS	RGB	Print, replay, 3D mask
WMCA George et al. [2019]	2019	72	6,716	RealSense/STC-PRO*	RGB/Depth/IR/Thermal	2 Print, replay, 2D/3D mask
CASIA-SURF Zhang et al. [2019b]	2018	1,000	21,000	RealSense	RGB/Depth/IR	Print, cut

1.2   BACKGROUND

1.2.1   DATASETS

Most of existing face anti-spoofing resources only consider the RGB modalitiy including Replay-Attack [Chingovska et al., 2012a] and CASIA-FASD [Zhang et al., 2012] datasets. The latter being two widely used datasets in PAD community. Even the recently released SiW [Liu et al., 2018] dataset is not the exception, despite the fact this dataset was collected with high resolution and image quality. With the widespread application of face recognition in mobile phones, there are also some RGB datasets recorded by replaying face video with smartphone or laptop, such as MSU-MFSD [Wen et al., 2015], Replay-Mobile [Costa-Pazo et al., 2016], and OULU-NPU [Boulkenafet et al., 2017b].

As attack techniques are changing constantly to adapt to security improvements, new types of presentation attacks (PAs) have emerged including 3D [Erdogmus and Marcel, 2014] and silicone masks [Bhattacharjee et al., 2018], which are more realistic than traditional 2D attacks. Therefore, the drawbacks of visible cameras are revealed when facing these realistic face masks. Fortunately, some new sensors have been introduced to provide more possibilities for face PAD methods, such as depth cameras, muti-spectral cameras, and infrared light cameras. Kim et al. [2009] aim to distinguish between the facial skin and mask materials by exploiting their reflectance. Kose and Dugelay [2013] propose a 2D + 3D face mask attacks dataset to study the effects of mask attacks, but the related dataset is not public. 3DMAD [Erdogmus and Marcel, 2014] is the first publicly available 3D masks dataset, which is recorded using Microsoft Kinect sensor and consists of the Depth and RGB modalities. Another multi-modal face PAD dataset is Msspoof [Chingovska et al., 2016] that contains visible (VIS) and near-infrared (NIR) images of real accesses and printed spoofing attacks with ≤ 21 objects.

However, these existing datasets in the face PAD community have two common limitations. On the one hand, they all comprise a limited number of subjects and samples, resulting in potential risk of over-fitting when face PAD algorithms are tested on these datasets [Chingovska et al., 2012a, Zhang et al., 2012]. On the other hand, most of the existing datasets are captured with a visible camera that only includes the RGB modality, causing a substantial portion of 2D PAD methods to fail when facing new types of PAs (3D and custom-made silicone masks). For the Chalearn LAP multi-modal face anti-spoofing attack detection challenge we released a novel dataset described in detail in Chapter 2. This dataset is the largest of its kind and comprises multiple modalities, over-comming the drawbacks of existing resources.

1.2.2   METHODS

Face anti-spoofing has been studied for decades now and great progress has been achieved recently in the field. In this section we briefly survey the most representative methodologies for approaching the problem. We mainly split the methods into two groups: traditional methods and deep learning-based methods.

Traditional Methods

Some previous works attempted to detect the evidence of *liveness* (e.g., eye-blinking) for detecting spoofing attacks [Bharadwaj et al., 2013, Kollreider et al., 2008, Pan et al., 2007, Wang et al., 2009]. Other works were based on contextual [Komulainen et al., 2013b, Pan et al., 2011] and motion [De Marsico et al., 2012, Kim et al., 2013, Wang et al., 2013] information. To improve the robustness to illumination variation, some algorithms have adopted HSV and YCbCr color spaces [Boulkenafet et al., 2016, 2017a], or worked on the Fourier spectrum [Li et al., 2004]. All of these methods have used handcrafted features, such as LBP [Chingovska et al., 2012b, Maatta et al., 2012, Ojala et al., 2002, Yang et al., 2013], HoG [Maatta et al., 2012, Schwartz et al., 2011, Yang et al., 2013], SIFT [Patel et al., 2016b], SURF [Boulkenafet et al., 2017a], DOG [Tan et al., 2010], and GLCM [Schwartz et al., 2011]. They are fast enough and have relatively satisfactory performance, but they have been evaluated only for in small publicly available face spoof datasets, hence they may have poor generalization capabilities.

Information fusion methods have been proposed trying to obtain a more general and effective countermeasure against a variation of attack types. Tronci et al. [2011] proposed a linear fusion at a frame and video level. Schwartz et al. [2011] introduced feature level fusion by using Partial Least Squares (PLS) regression based on a set of low-level feature descriptors. Some other works [de Freitas Pereira et al., 2013, Komulainen et al., 2013c] presented an effective fusion scheme by measuring the level of independence of two anti-counterfeiting systems. However, these fusion methods focus on score or feature level, and not on the modality level (i.e., the information that is combined comes from the same source), due to the lack of multi-modal datasets.

Deep Learning-Based Methods

Recently, deep learning-based methods have been introduced into the face PAD community. Some works [Feng et al., 2016, Li et al., 2016, Patel et al., 2016b, Yang et al., 2014] attempt to learn features by utilizing the convolutional neural networks (CNN) in an end-to-end manner. Concurrent to the supervision of using a softmax loss, some other works use auxiliary supervision module in CNN. Atoum et al. [2017] utilizes the face depth maps as supervisory information for the first time for face PAD. Then, Liu et al. [2018] design a novel CNN-RNN network architecture to leverage two auxiliary information (the Depth map and rPPG signal) as supervision with the goals of improving generalization. Shao et al. [2019] use depth as auxiliary supervision to learn invariant features for cross-domain face anti-spoofing. Jourabloo et al. [2018] introduce a new perspective for solving the face anti-spoofing by inversely decomposing a spoof face into the live face and the spoof noise pattern. Wang et al. [2020] take deep spatial gradient and temporal information to assist depth map regression and Yu et al. [2020] propose a novel frame-level FAS method based on Central Difference Convolution (CDC), which is able to capture intrinsic detailed patterns via aggregating both intensity and gradient information. Despite its competitive performance, these methodologies exhibit poor generalization capabilities during a cross-testing evaluation due to the small sample size.

With the goal of providing enough data for deep learning methodologies, and motivating the development of methods with better generalization capabilities, we released a large data set and organized a challenge around it. The next chapter introduces the CASIA-SURF data set and the remaining chapters present the results and the solutions developed by participants. As it can be seen below, novel and very effective methodologies have been developed in the context of this effort.

CHAPTER 2

Multi-Modal Face Anti-Spoofing Challenge

In this chapter, we first introduce CASIA-SURF the largest multi-modal dataset for the study of face anti-spoofing. Then, we briefly describe the challenge organized around this dataset.

2.1 CASIA-SURF DATASET

As previously mentioned in Chapter 1, all of existing datasets for face anti-spoofing detection involve fewer subjects and most of them consider a single modality. Although the publicly available datasets have driven the development of face PAD and continue to be valuable tools for this community, they have several limitations that hinder the development of face PAD in different ways. Particularly, there are still challenging problems under specific conditions that require higher recognition accuracy, e.g., face-based payment or unlocking of devices.

In order to address current limitations in PAD, we collected a new face PAD dataset, namely, the CASIA-SURF dataset. To the best our knowledge, CASIA-SURF is currently the largest face anti-spoofing dataset, containing 1,000 Chinese subjects in 21,000 videos. Another motivation in creating this dataset, beyond pushing the research on face anti-spoofing, is to explore recent face spoofing detection models performance when considering large-scale data. In the proposed dataset, each sample includes one live video clip, and six fake video clips under different attacks (one variety of attack per fake video clip). In the different attack styles, areas covering eyes, nose, mouth, or their combinations were cut from printed flat or curved facial images. As a result, six varieties of attacks were included in the CASIA-SURF dataset. The fake clips for a particular subject are illustrated in Fig. 2.1. Detailed information of the six attacks is given below.

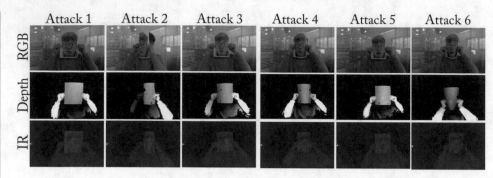

Figure 2.1: Six attack variants considered in the CASIA-SURF dataset.

- Attack 1: One person holds his/her flat face photo where eye regions are cut from the printed face.

- Attack 2: One person holds his/her curved face photo where eye regions are cut from the printed face.

- Attack 3: One person holds his/her flat face photo where eyes and nose regions are cut from the printed face.

- Attack 4: One person holds his/her curved face photo where eyes and nose regions are cut from the printed face.

- Attack 5: One person holds his/her flat face photo where eyes, nose, and mouth regions are cut from the printed face.

- Attack 6: One person holds his/her curved face photo where eyes, nose, and mouth regions are cut from the printed face.

2.1.1 ACQUISITION DETAILS

We used the Intel RealSense SR300 camera to capture the RGB, Depth, and Infrared (IR) videos simultaneously. In order to obtain the attack faces, we printed the color pictures of the collectors using A4 paper. During the video recording, the subjects were required to do some actions, such as turning left or right, moving up or down, walking in or away from the camera. Moreover, the face angle of performers were asked to be less than 30°. Performers stand within the range of 0.3–1.0 meters from the camera. The diagram of data acquisition procedure is

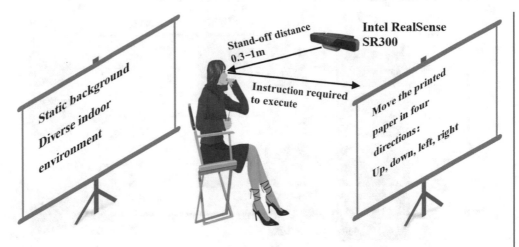

Figure 2.2: Illustrative sketch of recordings setups in the CASIA-SURF dataset.

shown in Fig. 2.2, showing how was it recorded the multi-modal data via Intel RealSence SR300 camera.

Four video streams including RGB, Depth, and IR images were captured at the same time, plus the RGB-Depth-IR aligned images using RealSense SDK. RGB, Depth, IR, and aligned images are shown in the first column of Fig. 2.3. The resolution is 1280×720 for RGB images, and 640×480 for Depth, IR and aligned images.

2.1.2   DATA PREPROCESSING

In order to make the dataset more challenging, we removed the complex background except face areas from original videos. Concretely, as shown in Fig. 2.3, the face area was obtained through the following steps. Although there is lack of face detection for Depth and IR face images, we have a RGB-Depth-IR aligned video clip for each sample. Therefore, we first use Dlib [King, 2009] to detect faces for every frame of RGB and RGB-Depth-IR aligned videos, respectively. The detected RGB and aligned faces are shown in the second column of Fig. 2.3. After face detection, we applied the PRNet [Feng et al., 2018] algorithm to perform 3D reconstruction and density alignment on the detected faces. The face area (namely, face reconstruction area) is shown in the third column of Fig. 2.3. Then, we defined a binary mask based on non-active face

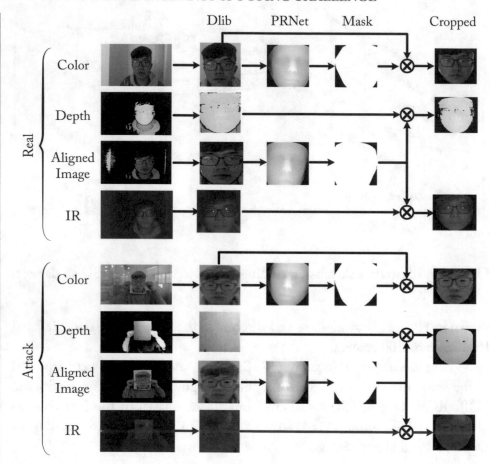

Figure 2.3: Preprocessing details of the three modalities of the CASIA-SURF dataset.

reconstruction area from previous step. The binary masks of RGB and RGB-Depth-IR images are shown in the fourth column of Fig. 2.3. Finally, we obtained face area of RGB image via pointwise product between RGB image and RGB binary mask. The Depth (or IR) area can be calculated via the pointwise product between Depth (or IR) image and RGB-Depth-IR binary mask. The face images of three modalities (RGB, Depth, IR) are shown in the last column of Fig. 2.3.

Table 2.1: Statistical information of the proposed CASIA-SURF dataset

	Training	Validation	Test	Total
# Objects	300	100	600	1,000
# Videos	6,300	2,100	12,600	21,000
# Original images	1,563,919	501,886	3,109,985	5,175,790
# Sample images	151,635	49,770	302,559	503,964
# Cropped images	148,089	48,789	295,644	492,522

2.1.3   STATISTICS

Table 2.1 presents the main statistics of the CASIA-SURF dataset. From such a table we can notice the following.

(1) There are 1,000 subjects and each one has a live video clip and 6 fake video clips. Data contain variability in terms of gender, age, glasses/no glasses, and indoor environments.

(2) Data are split in three sets: training, validation, and test. The training, validation, and test sets have 300, 100, and 600 subjects, respectively. Therefore, we can get 6,300 (2,100 per modality), 2,100 (700 per modality), and 12,600 (4,200 per modality) videos for its corresponding set.

(3) From original videos, there are about 1.5 million, 0.5 million, and 3.1 million frames in total for training, validation, and test sets, respectively. Owing to the huge amount of data, we select one frame out of every 10 frames and formed the sampled set with about 151K, 49K, and 302K for training, validation, and test sets, respectively.

(4) After data prepossessing in Section 2.1.2, by removing non-detected face poses with extreme lighting conditions, we finally get about 148K, 48K, and 295K frames for training, validation, and testing sets on the CASIA-SURF dataset, respectively.

All subjects are from China, and the information of gender statistics is shown on the left side of Fig. 2.4. This figure shows that the ratio of female is 56.8% while the ratio of male is 43.2%. In addition, we also show age distribution for the CASIA-SURF dataset on the right side of Fig. 2.4. One can see a wide distribution of age ranges from 20 to more than 70 years old, while most of subjects are under 70 years old. On average, the range of [20, 30) ages is dominant, being about 50% of all the subjects. A clear limitation of the dataset is

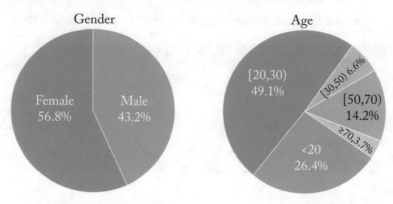

Figure 2.4: Statistical gender and age distribution of the CASIA-SURF dataset.

that it is biased in terms of ethnicity, we are working on extending this resource to include more diversity in this aspect.

2.1.4 EVALUATION PROTOCOL

Cross-testing. The cross-testing protocol uses the training set of CASIA-SURF to train the deep models, which are then fine-tuned on the target training dataset (e.g., the training set of SiW [Liu et al., 2018]). Finally, we test the fine-tuned model on the target test set (e.g., the test set of SiW [Liu et al., 2018]). The cross-testing protocol aims at simulating performance in real application scenarios involving high variabilities in appearance and having a limited number of samples to train the model.

Intra-testing. For the intra-testing protocol, information associated with real (live) faces and Attacks 4, 5, 6 was used for the training and validation sets. The training set is used to train the algorithm models while the validation set is used for model selection. Then, the live faces and Attacks 1, 2, 3 were used as the test set for final evaluation. This protocol is used for the evaluation of face anti-spoofing methods under controlled conditions, where training and test set belong to the CASIA-SURF dataset. The main reason for selecting the different attack types in the training and test set was to increase the difficulty of face anti-spoofing detection task. In the experiments section, we will show that there is still a big room for improvement under the ROC evaluation metric, especially, how to improve the true positive rate (TPR) at the little value of false positive rate (FAR), such as FAR $= 10^{-5}$.

2.2 CHALLENGE BASED ON THE CASIA-SURF DATASET

In this section, we briefly describe the organized challenge, including the evaluation metric and the challenge protocol. We relied on the CASIA-SURF dataset for the organization of the *ChaLearn Face Anti-spoofing Attack Detection Challenge*. Accordingly, the CASIA-SURF data set was processed as follows.

1. The dataset was split in three partitions: training, validation, and testing sets, with 300, 100, and 600 subjects, respectively. This partitioning corresponds to 6,300 (2,100 per modality), 2,100 (700 per modality), and 12,600 (4,200 per modality) videos for the corresponding partitions.

2. For each video, we retained 1 out every 10 frames to reduce its size. This subsampling strategy results in: 148K, 48K, and 295K frames for training, validation, and testing subsets, respectively.

3. The background except face areas from original videos was removed to increase the difficulty of the task.

Evaluation. In this challenge, we selected the recently standardized ISO/IEC 30107-3[1] metrics: Attack Presentation Classification Error Rate (APCER), Normal Presentation Classification Error Rate (NPCER), and Average Classification Error Rate (ACER) as the evaluation metrics. These are defined as follows:

$$APCER = FP/\left(FP + TN\right) \qquad (2.1)$$

$$NPCER = FN/\left(FN + TP\right) \qquad (2.2)$$

$$ACER = \left(APCER + NPCER\right)/2, \qquad (2.3)$$

where TP, FP, TN, and FN corresponds to true positive, false positive, true negative, and false negative, respectively. APCER and BPECER are used to measure the error rate of fake or live samples, respectively. Inspired by face recognition, the Receiver Operating Characteristic (ROC) curve is introduced for large-scale face anti-spoofing detection in CASIA-SURF dataset, which can be used to select a suitable threshold to trade off the false positive rate (FPR) and true positive rate (TPR) according to the requirements of real applications. Finally, the value TPR@FPR$= 10^{-4}$ was the leading evaluation measure for

[1]https://www.iso.org/obp/ui/iso

this challenge. APCER, NPCER, and ACER measures were used as additional evaluation criteria.

Challenge protocol. The challenge was run in the CodaLab[2] platform, and comprised two stages as follows.

Development Phase: (*Started: Dec. 22, 2018–Ended: in March 6, 2019*). During this phase participants had access to labeled training data and unlabeled validation samples. Participants could use training data to develop their models, and they could submit predictions on the validation partition. Training data were made available with samples labeled with the genuine and three forms of attack (4,5,6). Whereas samples in the validation partition were associated with genuine and three different attacks (1,2,3). For the latter dataset, labels were not made available to participants. Instead, participants could submit predictions on the validation partition and receive immediate feedback via the leader board. The main reason for including different attack types in the training and validation dataset was to increase the difficulty of FAD challenge.

Final phase: (*Started: March 6, 2019–Ended: March 10, 2019*). During this phase, labels for the validation subset were made available to participants, so that they can have more labeled data for training their models. The unlabeled testing set was also released, participants had to make predictions for the testing partition and upload their solutions to the challenge platform. The considered test set was formed by examples labeled with the genuine label and three attack types (1,2,3). Participants had the opportunity to make three submissions for the final phase, this was done with the goal of assessing stability of their methods. Note that the CodaLab platform defaults to the result of the last submission.

The final ranking of participants was obtained from the performance of submissions in the testing sets. To be eligible for prizes, winners had to publicly release their code under a license of their choice and provide a fact sheet describing their solution.

2.3   DATASET APPLICATION

We cooperated with a startup SurfingTech,[3] which helped us to collect the face anti-spoofing data. This company focuses on data collection, data label-

---

[2]https://competitions.codalab.org
[3]http://surfing.ai/

ing, as well as it sells collected data with accurate labels. All participants had a monetary compensation and signed an agreement to make data public for academic research. If the industry company wants to use it, it has to buy the source data from SurfingTech. If you interested in this dataset, you can apply it in the link https://sites.google.com/qq.com/face-anti-spoofing/dataset-download/casia-surfcvpr2019.

CHAPTER 3

Review of Participants' Methods

This section describes the top-ranked solutions developed in the context of the ChaLearn Face Anti-spoofing attack detection challenge. Additionally, we also describe the baseline which we have developed for the competition.

3.1 BASELINE METHOD

We developed a strong baseline method associated with the challenge. Our aim was to provide a straightforward architecture achieving competitive performance in the CASIA-SURF dataset. In doing this, we approached the face anti-spoofing problem as a binary classification task (fake vs. real) and conducted experiments using the ResNet-18 [He et al., 2016] classification network. ResNet-18 consists of five convolutional blocks (namely **res1, res2, res3, res4, res5**), a global average pooling layer, and a softmax layer, which is a relatively shallow network but has strong classification capabilities.

3.1.1 NAIVE HALFWAY FUSION

As described before, the CASIA-SURF dataset is characterized for being multimodal (i.e., RGB, Depth, IR) and one of the main problems to solve is how to fuse the complementary information from the three available modalities. For the baseline, we use a multi-stream architecture with three subnetworks where RGB, Depth, and IR data are processed separately by each stream, and then shared layers are appended at a point to learn joint representations and decisions. Halfway fusion is one of the commonly used fusion methods, which combines the subnetworks of different modalities at a later stage, i.e., immediately after the third convolutional block (res3) via the feature map concatenation (similar to Fig. 3.1, except no "Squeeze-and-Excitation" fusion). In this way, features from different modalities can be fused to perform classification. However, direct

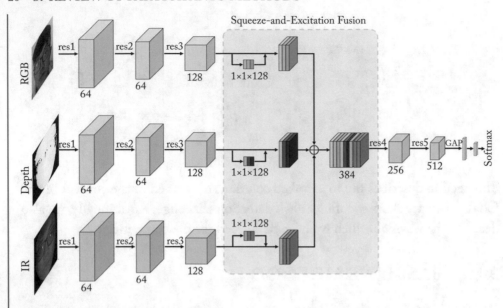

Figure 3.1: Diagram of the proposed method. Each stream uses the ResNet-18 as the backbone, which has five convolutional blocks (i.e., res1, res2, res3, res4, res5). The res1, res2, and res3 blocks are proprietary to extract features of each modal data (i.e., RGB, Depth, IR). Then, these features from different modalities are fused via the squeeze and excitation fusion module. After that, the res4 and res5 blocks are shared to learn more discriminatory features from the fused one. GAP means the global average pooling.

concatenating these features cannot make full use of the characteristics between different modalities by itself.

3.1.2   SQUEEZE AND EXCITATION FUSION

Since different modalities have different characteristics, the RGB information has rich visual details, the Depth data are sensitive to the distance between the image plane and the corresponding face, and the IR data measure the amount of heat radiated from a face. These three modalities have different advantages and disadvantages for different ways of attack. Inspired by Hu et al. [2018a], we proposed the squeeze and excitation fusion method that uses the "Squeeze-and-Excitation" branch to enhance the representational ability of the different modalities' features by explicitly modeling the interdependencies between their convolutional channels.

As shown in Fig. 3.1, our squeeze and excitation fusion method has a three-stream architecture and each subnetwork is feed with the image of different modalities. The res1, res2, and res3 blocks are proprietary for each stream to extract the features of different modalities. After that, these features are fused via the squeeze and excitation fusion module. This module newly adds a branch for each modal and the branch is composed of one global average pooling layer and two consecutive fully connected (FC) layers. The squeeze and excitation fusion module performs modal-dependent feature re-weighting to select the more informative channel features while suppress less useful ones for each modal, and then concatenates these re-weighted features to the fused feature. In this way, we can make full use of the characteristics between different modalities via re-weighting their features.

3.2   PARTICIPANTS' METHODS

This section describes the solutions developed by top-ranked participants [Parkin and Grinchuk, 2019, Shen et al., 2019, Zhang et al., 2019a] of the ChaLearn face anti-spoofing attack detection challenge.

3.2.1   1ST PLACE (TEAM NAME: VISIONLABS)

Attack Specific Folds. Because attack types at test time can differ from attacks presented in the training set, in order to increase the robustness to new attacks, Parkin and Grinchuk [2019] splits training data into three folds. Each fold contains two different attacks, while images of the third attack type are used for validation. Once trained, one treats three different networks as a single model by averaging their prediction scores.

Transfer Learning. Many image recognition tasks with limited training data benefit from CNN pre-training on large-scale image datasets, such as ImageNet [Deng et al., 2009]. Fine tuning network parameters that have been pre-trained on various source tasks leads to different results on the target task. In the experiments, Parkin and Grinchuk [2019] use four datasets designed for face recognition and gender classification (please see Table 3.1), to generate a useful and promising initialization. They also use multiple backbone ResNet architectures and losses for initial tasks to increase the variability. Similar to

Table 3.1: Face datasets and the CNN architecture are used to pre-train the networks of VisionLabs [Parkin and Grinchuk, 2019]

	Backbone	Dataset	Task
1	ResNet-34	CASIA-Web face [Yi et al., 2014]	Face recognition
2	ResNet-34	AFAD-lite [Niu et al., 2016]	Gender classification
3	ResNet-50	MSCeleb-1M [Guo et al., 2016]	Face recognition
4	ResNet-50	Asian dataset [Zhao et al., 2018]	Face recognition

networks trained for attack-specific folds in the last paragraph, authors average predictions of all the models trained with different initializations.

Model Architecture. The final network architecture is based on the ResNet-34 and ResNet-50 backbone with SE modules which are illustrated in Fig. 3.2. Following the method described in our baseline method [Zhang et al., 2019b], each modality is processed by the first three residual convolutional blocks, then the output features are fused using squeeze and excitation fusion module and processed by the remaining residual block. Differently from the baseline method, Parkin and Grinchuk [2019] enrich the model with additional aggregation blocks at each feature level. Each aggregation block takes features from the corresponding residual blocks and from previous aggregation block, making the model capable of finding inter-modal correlations not only at a fine level but also at a coarse one. In addition, it trains each model using two initial random seeds. Given separate networks for attack-specific folds and different pre-trained models, our final liveness score is obtained by averaging the outputs of 24 neural network.

Conclusions. The solution proposed by Parkin and Grinchuk [2019] achieved the top 1 rank at the Chalearn LAP face anti-spoofing challenge. First, authors have demonstrated that careful selection of a training subset by the types of spoofing samples better generalizes to unseen attacks. Second, they have proposed a multi-level feature aggregation module which fully utilizes the feature fusion from different modalities both at coarse and fine levels. Finally, authors have examined the influence of feature transfer from different pre-trained models on the target task and showed that using the ensemble of various face-related tasks as source domains increases the stability and the per-

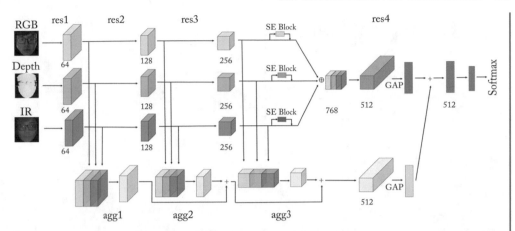

Figure 3.2: The proposed architecture (VisionLabs). RGB, IR, and Depth streams are processed separately using res1, res2, res3 blocks from resnet-34 as a backbone. The res3 output features are re-weighted and fused via the squeeze and excitation (SE) block and then fed into res4. In addition, branch features from res1, res2, res3 are concatenated and processed by corresponding aggregation blocks, each aggregation block also uses information from the previous one. The resulting features from agg3 are fed into res4 and summed up with the features from the modality branch. On the diagram: GAP—global average pooling; ⊕ concatenation; +—elementwise addition.

formance of the system. The code and pre-trained models are publicly available from the github repository at https://github.com/AlexanderParkin/ChaLearn_liveness_challenge. More information of this method can be found in Parkin and Grinchuk [2019].

3.2.2 2ND PLACE (TEAM NAME: READSENSE)

The Overall Architecture. In this work, Shen et al. [2019] proposed a multistream CNN architecture called FaceBagNet with Modal Feature Erasing (MFE) for multi-modal face anti-spoofing detection. The proposed Face-BagNet consists of two components: (1) patch-based features learning and (2) multi-stream fusion with MFE. For the patch-based features learning, Shen et al. [2019] trained a deep neural network by using patches randomly extracted from face images to learn rich appearance features. For the multi-stream fusion, features from different modalities are randomly erased during training, which

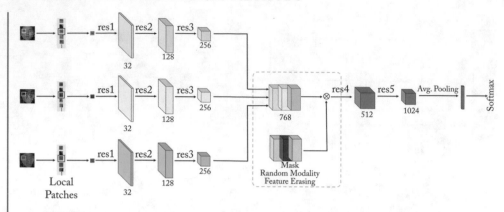

Figure 3.3: The proposed architecture (ReadSense). The fusion network is trained from scratch in which RGB, Depth, and IR face patches are feed into it at the same time. Image augmentation is applied and modal features from sub-network are randomly erased during training.

are then fused to perform classification. Figure 3.3 shows the high-level illustration of three streams along with a fusion strategy for combining them.

Patch-based Features Learning. The spoof-specific discriminative information exists in the whole face area. Therefore, Shen et al. [2019] used the patch-level image to enforce convolution neural network to extract such information. The usual patch-based approaches split the full face into several fixed non-overlapping regions. Then each patch is used to train an independent sub-network. For each modality, Shen et al. [2019] trained one single CNN on random patches extracted from the faces. Then authors used a self-designed ResNext [Xie et al., 2017] network to extract deep features. The network consisted of five group convolutional blocks, a global average pooling layer, and a softmax layer. Table 3.2 presents the network architecture in terms of its layers, i.e., size of kernels, number of output feature maps, and number of groups and strides.

Multi-stream Fusion With MFE. Since the feature distributions of different modalities are different, the proposed model makes efforts to exploit the interdependencies between different modalities as well. As shown in Fig. 3.3, it uses a multi-stream architecture with three sub-networks to perform multi-

Table 3.2: Architecture of the proposed FaceBagNet [Shen et al., 2019]

Patch Size	Configuration
Layer 1	Conv 3 × 3, 32
Layer 2	[Conv 1 × 1, 64 Conv 3 × 3, 64, Group 32, Stride 2 Conv 1 × 1, 128] × 2
Layer 3	[Conv 1 × 1, 128 Conv 3 × 3, 128, Group 32, Stride 2 Conv 1 × 1, 256] × 2
Layer 4	[Conv 1 × 1, 256 Conv 3 × 3, 256, Group 32, Stride 2 Conv 1 × 1, 512] × 2
Layer 5	[Conv 1 × 1, 512 Conv 3 × 3, 512, Group 32, Stride 2 Conv 1 × 1, 1024] × 2
Layer 6	Global average pooling FC2

modal features fusion. Then authors concatenated feature maps of three sub-networks after the third convolutional block (res3).

As studied in our baseline method [Zhang et al., 2019b], directly concatenating features from each sub-network cannot make full use of the characteristics between different modalities. In order to prevent overfitting and for better learning the fusion features, Shen et al. [2019] designed a Modal Feature Erasing (MFE) operation on the multi-modal features. For one batch of inputs, the concatenated feature tensor is computed by three sub networks. During training, the features from one randomly selected modal sub-network are erased and the corresponding units inside the erased area are set to zero. The fusion network is trained from scratch in which RGB, Depth, and IR data are fed separately into each sub-network at the same time.

Conclusions. Shen et al. [2019] proposed a face anti-spoofing network based on Bag-of-local-features (named FaceBagNet) to determine whether the captured multi-modal face images are real. A patch-based feature learning method was used to extract discriminative information. Multi-stream fusion with MFE layer was applied to improve the performance. It demonstrated that both patch-based feature learning method and multi-stream fusion with MFE were effective methods for face anti-spoofing. Overall, the proposed solution was simple but effective and easy to use in practical application scenarios. As the result, the proposed approach [Shen et al., 2019] obtained the second place in CVPR 2019 ChaLearn Face Anti-spoofing attack detection challenge.

3.2.3   3RD PLACE (TEAM NAME: FEATHER)

The existing face anti-spoofing networks [Hernandez-Ortega et al., 2018, Li et al., 2016, Patel et al., 2016a, Wang et al., 2018] have the problems of large parameters and weak generalization ability. For this reason, Zhang et al. [2019a] proposed a FeatherNets architecture, because of this network is light as a feather.

The Weakness of GAP for Face Task. Global Average Pooling (GAP) is employed by a lot of state-of-the-art networks for object recognition task, such as ResNets [He et al., 2016], DenseNet [Huang et al., 2017b], and some light-weight networks, like MobilenetV2 [Sandler et al., 2018], and Shuf-flenet_v2 [Ma et al., 2018], IGCV3 [Sun et al., 2018]. GAP has been proved on its ability of reducing dimensions and preventing over-fitting for the over-all structure [Lin et al., 2013]. For the face related tasks, Wu et al. [2018a] and Deng et al. [2019] have observed that CNNs with GAP layer are less accurate than those without GAP. Meanwhile, MobileFaceNet [Chen et al., 2018] replaces the GAP with Global Depthwise Convolution (GDConv) layer, and explains the reason why it is effective through the theory of receptive field [Long et al., 2014]. The main point of GAP is "equal importance" which is not suitable for face tasks.

As shown in Fig. 3.4, the last 7×7 feature map is denoted as FMap-end, each cell in FMap-end corresponds to a receptive field at different position. The center blue cell corresponds to RF1 and the edge red one corresponds to RF2. As described in Luo et al. [2016], the distribution of impact in a receptive field distributes as a Gaussian, the center of a receptive field has more impact on the output than the edge. Therefore, RF1 has larger effective receptive field than RF2. For the face anti-spoofing task, the network input is 224×224 images which only contain the face region. As in the above analysis, the center unit of FMap-end is more important than the edge one. GAP is not applicable to this

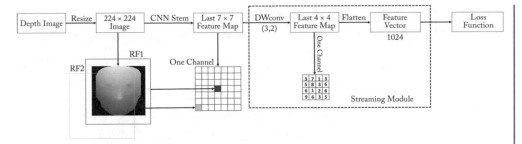

Figure 3.4: Depth faces feature embedding CNN structure. In the last 7×7 feature map, the receptive field and the edge (RF2) portion of the middle part (RF1) is different, because their importance is different. DWConv is used instead of the GAP layer to better identify this different importance. At the same time, the FC layer is removed, which makes the network more portable. This figure is from Zhang et al. [2019a].

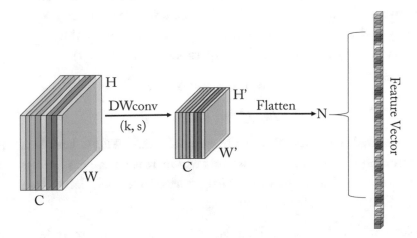

Figure 3.5: Streaming Module. The last blocks' output is down-sampled by a depthwise convolution [Chollet, 2017, Howard et al., 2017] with stride larger than 1 and flattened directly into a 1D vector.

case. One choice is to use FC layer instead of GAP. It would introduce a large number of parameters to the whole model and increase the risk of over-fitting.

Streaming Module. To treat different units of FMap-end with different importance, streaming module is designed which is shown in Fig. 3.5. In streaming module, a depthwise convolution (DWConv) layer with stride larger than 1 is used for down-sampling whose output, is then flattened directly into an 1D feature vector. The compute process is represented by Equation (3.1):

$$FV_{n(y,x,m)} = \sum_{i,j} K_{i,j,m} \cdot F_{IN_y(i),IN_x(j),m} \qquad (3.1)$$

In Equation (3.1), FV is the flattened feature vector while $N = H' \times W' \times C$ elements (H', W', and C denote the height, width, and channel of DWConv layer's output feature maps, respectively). $n(y,x,m)$, computed as Equation (3.2), denotes the nth element of FV which corresponds to the (y,x) unit in the mth channel of the DWConv layer's output feature maps:

$$n(y,x,m) = m \times H' \times W' + y \times H' + x \qquad (3.2)$$

On the right side of Equation (3.1), K is the depthwise convolution kernel and F is the FMap-end of size H × W × C (H, W, and C denote the height, width, and channel of FMap-end, respectively). m denotes the channel index. i,j denote the spatial position in kernel K, and $IN_y(i)$, $IN_x(j)$ denote the corresponding position in F. They are computed as Equations (3.3) and (3.4):

$$IN_y(i) = y \times S_0 + i \qquad (3.3)$$

$$IN_x(j) = x \times S_1 + j \qquad (3.4)$$

S_0 is the vertical stride and S_1 is the horizontal stride. An FC layer is not added after flattening feature map, because this will increase more parameters and the risk of overfitting. Streaming module can be used to replace global average pooling and FC layer in traditional networks.

Network Architecture Details. Besides streaming module, there are BlockA/B/C, as shown in Fig. 3.6, to compose FeatherNetA/B. The detailed structure of the primary FeatherNet architecture is shown in Table 3.3. **BlockA** is the inverted residual blocks proposed in MobilenetV2 [Sandler et al., 2018]. BlockA is used as our main building block which is shown in Fig. 3.6a. The expansion factors are the same as in MobilenetV2 [Sandler et al., 2018] for blocks in our architecture. **BlockB** is the down-sampling module of FeatherNetB. Average pooling (AP) has been proved in Inception [Szegedy et al., 2015] to benefit performance, because of its ability of embedding multi-scale information and aggregating features in different receptive fields. Therefore, average pooling (2 × 2 kernel with stride = 2) is introduced in BlockB (Fig. 3.6b). Besides,

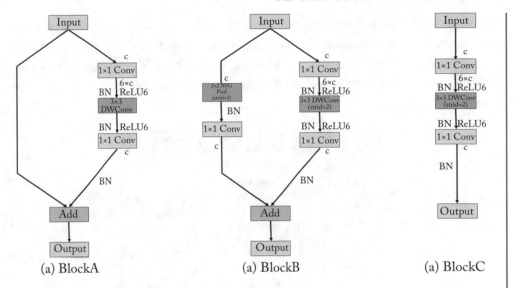

Figure 3.6: FeatherNets' main blocks. FeatherNetA includes BlockA and BlockC. FeatherNetB includes BlockA and BlockB. (BN: BatchNorm; DW-Conv: depth wise convolution; c:number of input channels.)

in the network ShuffleNet [Ma et al., 2018], the down-sampling module joins 3×3 average pooling layer with stride=2 to obtain excellent performance. Li et al. [Xie et al., 2018] suggested that increasing average pooling layer works well and impacts the computational cost little. Based on the above analysis, adding pooling on the secondary branch can learn more diverse features and bring performance gains. **BlockC** is the down-sampling Module of our network FeatherNetA. BlockC is faster and with less complexity than BlockB.

After each down-sampling stage, SE-module [Hu et al., 2018b] is inserted with reduce = 8 in both FeatherNetA and FeatherNetB. In addition, when designing the model, a fast down-sampling strategy [Qin et al., 2018] is used at the beginning of our network which makes the feature map size decrease rapidly and without much parameters. Adopting this strategy can avoid the problem of weak feature embedding and high processing time caused by slow down-sampling due to limited computing budget [Duong et al., 2018]. The primary FeatherNet only has 0.35M parameters.

The FeatherNets' structure is built on BlockA/B/C, as mentioned above, except for the first layer which is a fully connected. As shown in Table 3.3, the

Table 3.3: Network Architecture: FeatherNet B. All spatial convolutions use 3 × 3 kernels. The expansion factor t is always applied to the input size, while c means number of Channel. Meanwhile, every stage SE-module [Hu et al., 2018b] is inserted with reduce = 8. And FeatherNetA replaces BlockB in the table with BlockC.

Input	Operator	t	c
$224^2 \times 3$	Conv2d,/2	–	32
$112^2 \times 32$	BlockB	1	16
$56^2 \times 16$	BlockB	6	32
$28^2 \times 32$	BlockA	6	32
$28^2 \times 32$	BlockB	6	48
$14^2 \times 48$	5 × BlockA	6	48
$14^2 \times 48$	BlockB	6	64
$7^2 \times 64$	2 × BlockA	6	64
$7^2 \times 64$	Streaming	–	1024

size of the input image is 224 × 224. A layer with regular convolutions, instead of depthwise convolutions, is used at the beginning to keep more features. Reuse channel compression to reduce 16 while using inverted residuals and linear bottleneck with expansion ratio = 6 to minimize the loss of information due to down-sampling. Finally, the Streaming module is used without adding an FC layer, directly flatten the 4 × 4 × 64 feature map into an 1D vector, reducing the risk of over-fitting caused by the FC layer. After flattening the feature map, focal loss is used directly for prediction.

Multi-Modal Fusion Method. The main idea for the fusion method is to use a cascade inference on different modalities: depth images and IR images. The cascade structure has two stages, shown in Fig. 3.7.

Stage 1: An ensemble classifier, consisting of multiple models, is employed to generate the predictions. These models are trained on depth data and from several checkpoints of different networks, including FeatherNets. If the weighted average of scores from these models is near 0 or 1, input sample will be classified as fake or real, respectively. Otherwise, the uncertain samples will go through the second stage.

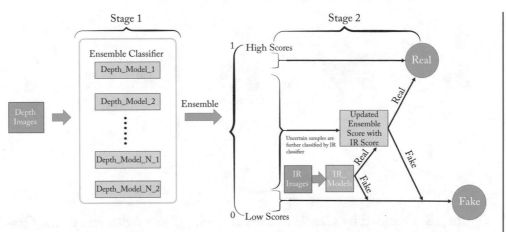

Figure 3.7: Multi-Modal Fusion Strategy: two stages cascaded. Stage 1 is an ensemble classifier consisting of several depth models. Stage 2 employs IR models to classify the uncertain samples from Stage 1.

Stage 2: FeatherNetB learned from IR data will be used to classify the uncertain samples from Stage 1. The fake judgment of IR model is respected as the final result. For the real judgment, the final scores are decided by both stage 1 and IR models.

   Conclusions. It proposes an extreme light network architecture (FeatherNet A/B) with Streaming module, to achieve a good trade-off between performance and computational complexity for multi-modal face anti-spoofing. Furthermore, a novel fusion classifier with "ensemble + cascade" structure is proposed for the performance preferred use cases. Meanwhile, CASIA-SURF dataset [Zhang et al., 2019b] is collected to provide more diverse samples and more attacks to gain better generalization ability. All these are used to join the Face Anti-spoofing Attack Detection Challenge@CVPR2019 and get the third place in this challenge.

3.2.4   OTHER TEAMS

Hahahaha. Their base model is a Resnext [Xie et al., 2017] which was pretrained with the ImageNet dataset [Deng et al., 2009]. Then, they fine tune the network on aligned images with face landmark and use data augmentation to strengthen the generalization ability.

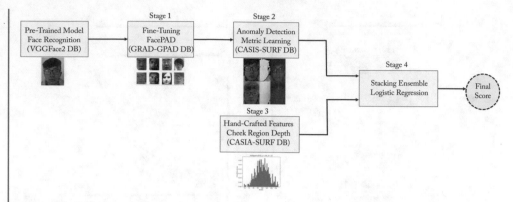

Figure 3.8: Provided by GradiantResearch team. General diagram of the GradiantResearch team.

MAC-adv-group. This solution used the Resnet-34 [He et al., 2016] as base network. To overcome the influence of illumination variation, they convert RGB image to HSV color space. Then, they sent the features extracted from the network into an FC layer and a binary classification layer.

ZKBH. Analyzing the training, validation, and test sets, participants assumed that the eye region is promising to get good performance in an FAD task based on an observation that the eye region is the common attack area. After several trials, the input of the final version they submitted adopted quarter face containing the eye region. Different from prior works that regard the face anti-spoofing problem as merely a binary (fake vs. real) classification problem, this team constructed a regression model for differentiating the real face and the attacks.

VisionMiracle. This solution was based on the modified shufflenet-V2 [Ma et al., 2018]. The feature-map was divided into two branches after the third stage, and connected in the fourth stage.

GradiantResearch. The fundamental idea behind this solution was the reformulation of the face presentation attack detection problem (face-PAD) following an anomaly detection strategy using deep metric learning. The approach can be split in four stages (Fig. 3.8).

Stage 1: Use a pre-trained model for face recognition and apply a classification-like metric learning approach in GRAD-GPAD dataset [Costa-Pazo et al., 2019] using only RGB images.

Stage 2: They fine tune the model obtained in Stage 1 with the CASIA-SURF dataset using metric learning for anomaly detection (semi-hard batch negative mining with triplet focal loss) adding Depth and IR images to the input volume. Once the model converged, they trained an SVM classifier using the features of the last FC layer (128D).

Stage 3: They trained an SVM classifier using the normalized histogram of the depth image corresponding to the cheek region of the face (256D).

Stage 4: They performed a simple stacking ensemble of both models (Stages 2 and 3) by training a logistic regression model with the scores in the training split.

Vipl-bpoic. This team focused on improving face anti-spoofing generalization ability by proposing an end-to-end trainable face anti-spoofing model with attention mechanism. Due to the sample imbalance, they assign the weight of 1:3 according to the number of genuine and spoof faces in Training set. Subsequently, they fuse the three modal images including RGB, Depth, and IR into five channels as the input of ResNet-18 [He et al., 2016] which integrated with the convolutional block attention module. The center loss [Wen et al., 2016] and cross-entropy loss are adopted to constrain the learning process in order to get more discriminative cues of FAD finally.

Massyhnu. This team paid attention to color information fusion and ensemble learning [Peng et al., 2018a,b].

AI4all. This team used VGG16 [Simonyan and Zisserman, 2014] as the backbone for face PAD.

Guillaume. Their method consists in a Multi-Channel convolutional Neural Network (MC-CNN) taking a face images of different modalities as input. Near-infrared and depth images only have been used in their approach. The architecture of the proposed MC-CNN is based on the second version of the LightCNN [Wu et al., 2018b] containing 29 layers. Also, the pretrained LightCNN model is used as a starting point for their training procedure. The training consists in the fine-tuning of the low-level convolutional layers of the network in each modalities, and in learning the final FC layers.

3.2.5   SUMMARY

For the organized face anti-spoofing challenge@CVPR 2020 workshop, no team used traditional methods for FAD, such as detecting physiological signs of life, eye blinking, facial expression changes, and mouth movements. Instead, all submitted face PAD solutions relied on model-based feature extractors, such as ResNet [He et al., 2016], VGG16 [Simonyan and Zisserman, 2014], etc.

A summary is provided in Table 3.4. All teams use the deep learning-based methods with or without pretrained models from other dataset (such as face dataset used in both VisionLabs and GradiantResearch teams) and only the Feather Team use the private FAD data. The teames of top three are used at least two modalities (RGB, Depth, or IR). Interesting, the Hahahaha team only use the depth modality but also obtained very promising results. The details of performances among participant teams are summarized in the next chapter.

Table 3.4: Summary of the methods for all participating teams. Information on the detailed performance of these methods can be found in Table 4.10. (*Continues.*)

Rank	Team Name	Method	Model	Pre-Trained Data	Modality	Pre-Process	Additional FAD Dataset	Fusion and Loss Function
1	VisionLabs	Fine-tuning Ensembling	ResNet34 ResNet50	CASIA-WebFace AFAD-Lite MSCeleb1M Asian dataset	RGB Depth IR	Resize	No	Squeeze and Excitation Fusion Score Fusion Softmax
2	ReadSense	Bag of features Ensembling	SEResnext	No	RGB Depth IR	Crop image Data aug.	No	Squeeze and Excitation Fusion Score Fusion Softmax
3	Feather	Ensembling	Fishnet MobileNetv2	No	Depth IR	Resize Image adjust	Private FAD data	Score Fusion Softmax
4	Hahahaha	Fine-tuning	Resnext	Imagenet	Depth	Data aug. Aligned faces	No	Softmax
5	MAC-Adv-Group	Fusion	ResNet34	No	RGB Depth IR	Transfer learning Color space	No	Feature fusion Softmax
6	ZKBH	Regression model	REsNet18	No	RGB Depth IR	Crop image Data aug.	No	Data fusion Regression loss
7	VisionMiracle	Modified CNN	Shufflenet-v2	No	Depth	Data aug.	No	Softmax
8	Baseline	Feature fusion	REsNet18	No	RGB Depth IR	Resize Data aug.	No	Softmax

Table 3.4: (*Continues.*) Summary of the methods for all participating teams. Information on the detailed performance of these methods can be found in Table 4.10.

7	VisionMiracle	Modified CNN	Shufflenet-v2	No	Depth	Data aug.	No	Softmax
					RGB	Resize		
8	Baseline	Feature fusion	REsNet18	No	Depth		No	Softmax
					IR	Data aug.		
				VGGFace2	RGB	Crop image		Ensemble
9	Gradi-antResearch	Metric learning	Inception ResNet v1		Depth		No	
				GRAD-GPAD	IR	Data aug.		Logistic regression
					RGB	Ratio of positive		Data fusion
10	Vipl-bpoic	Attention mechanics	REsNet18	No	Depth	and negative	No	Center loss
					IR			Softmax
					RGB			Fusion
11	Massyhnu	Ensembling	9 classifiers	No	Depth	Resize	No	
					IR	Transfer color space		Softmax
12	AI4all	Depth image	VGG16	No	Depth	Resize, Data aug.	No	Softmax
					Depth			Data fusion
13	Guillaume	Multi-channel CNN	LightCNN	Yes	IR	Resize	No	Softmax

CHAPTER 4

Challenge Results

In this chapter, the results obtained by the thirteen teams that qualified to the final phase of the challenge are presented. We first present the performance of the top three teams [Parkin and Grinchuk, 2019, Shen et al., 2019, Zhang et al., 2019a]. Then, the effectiveness of proposed algorithms are analyzed and we point out some limitations of the algorithms proposed by participating teams. Please note that the evaluation metrics used for the challenge were introduced in Section 2.1.4.

4.1 EXPERIMENTS

In this section, we present the performance obtained by the top three teams. It illustrates the detail implementation details, pre-processing strategy and results on the CASIA-SURF dataset.

4.1.1 1ST PLACE (TEAM NAME: VISIONLABS)

The architecture of VisonLabs has been presented in Section 3.2.1, where three branches and fusion strategy of RGB, Depth, and IR images are applied. Readers can refer to Section 3.2.1 for more detailed method of VisionLabs. Here, we only provide the experimental results of VisionLabs.

Implementation Details

All the code was implemented in PyTorch [Paszke et al., 2017] and models were trained on 4 NVIDIA 1080Ti cards. Single model trains about 3 hours and the inference takes 8 seconds per 1,000 images. All neural nets were trained using ADAM [12] with cosine learning rate strategy and optimized for standard cross entropy loss for two classes. It trained each model for 30 epochs with initial learning rate at 0.1 with batch size of 128.

Table 4.1: Results on CASIA-SURF validation subset

Method	Initialization	Fold	TPR@FPR=10^{-4}
[Zhang et al., 2019b]			56.80
ResNet18		Subject 5-fold	60.54
ResNet34		Subject 5-fold	74.55
ResNet34		Attack 3-fold	78.89
ResNet34	ImageNet	Attack 3-fold	92.12
ResNet34	CASIA-Webface	Attack 3-fold	99.80
A. ResNet34 with MLFA	CASIA-Webface	Attack 3-fold	99.87
B. ResNet50 with MLFA	MSCeleb-1M	Attack 3-fold	99.63
C. ResNet50 with MLFA	ASIAN dataset	Attack 3-fold	99.33
D. ResNet34 with MLFA	AFAD-lite	Attack 3-fold	98.70
A, B, C, D ensemble		Attack 3-fold	100.00

Preprocessing

CASIA-SURF already provides face crops so no detection algorithms were used to align images. Face crops were resized to 125×125 pixels and then center crop 112×112 was taken. At the training stage horizontal flip was applied with 0.5 probability. Parkin and Grinchuk [2019] also tested different crop and rotation strategies as well as test-time augmentation, however, this did not result in significant improvements and no additional augmentation was used in the final model except the above.

Baseline

Unless mentioned explicitly, results on Chalearn LAP challenge validation set are reported as obtained from the Codalab evaluation platform. First of all, VisionLabs reproduced baseline method [Zhang et al., 2019b] with Resnet-18 backbone and trained it using a 5-fold cross-validation strategy. All folds are split are reported based on the subject identity so images from the same person belong only to one fold. Then the score is averaged for the five trained nets and TPR@FPR= 10^{-4} is reported in Table 4.1. The resulting performance is close to perfect and similar to the previously reported results in Zhang et al. [2019b], which was calculated on the test set. The test set differs from the validation, but belongs to the same spoofing attack distribution.

Next, Visionlab [Parkin and Grinchuk, 2019] expand the backbone architecture to ResNet34 which would improve the score by a large margin. Due to the GPU limitations, VisionLabs further focus only on ResNet34 and add Resnet50 only at the final stage.

Attack-Specific Folds

Here, VisionLabs [Parkin and Grinchuk, 2019] compared the 5-fold split strategy based on subject IDs with the strategy based on spoof attack types. Real examples by subject identity were assigned randomly to the one of the three folds.

Despite the fact that the new model computes an average of three network outputs while each of these networks was trained on less data compared to the subject 5-fold learning strategy, the trained model achieves better performance compared to the baseline method (see Table 4.1). VisionLabs [Parkin and Grinchuk, 2019] explained this by the improved generalization to new attacks due to the training for different types of attacks.

Initialization Matters

In the next experiment, VisionLabs [Parkin and Grinchuk, 2019] initializes each of the three modality branches of the network with the res1, res2, res3 blocks from the ImageNet pre-trained network. The Fusion SE parts are left unchanged and the final res4 block is also initialized by the ImageNet pre-trained weights. Finetuning of this model on the CASIA-SURF dataset gives significant improvement over networks with random initialization (see Table 4.1). Moreover, switching pre-training to the face recognition task on the CASIA-WebFace dataset [Yi et al., 2014] improves results by even a larger margin and reaches almost perfect TPR of 99.80%.

Multi-Level Feature Aggregation

Here, VisionLabs [Parkin and Grinchuk, 2019] examine the effect of multi-level feature aggregation (MLFA) described in the model architecture section. The results are shown in Table 4.1. It initializes aggregation modules with random weights and train the new architecture following the best learning protocol.

The ResNet34 network with MLFA blocks has demonstrated error reduction by the factor 1.5x compared to the network without MFLA blocks.

Ensembling

To improve the stability of the solution, VisionLabs uses four face-related datasets as an inialization for the final model. It used publicly available networks with weights trained for face recognition tasks on the CASIA-WebFace [Yi et al., 2014], MSCeleb-1M [Guo et al., 2016], and private Asian faces [Zhao et al., 2018]. One also trained a network for gender classification on the AFADlite [Niu et al., 2016] dataset. Different tasks, losses, and datasets imply different convolutional features and the average prediction of models fine tuned with such initializations leads to 100.00% TPR@FPR= 10^{-4}.

Such a high score meets the requirements of real-world security applications, however, it was achieved using a large number of ensembling networks. In future work, VisionLabs plans to focus on reducing the size of the model and making it applicable for the real-time execution.

Solution Stability

The consistency and stability of model performance on unseen data is important especially when it comes to real-world security applications. During the validation phase of the challenge seven teams achieved perfect or near perfect accuracy, however only three solutions managed to hold close level of performance on the test set (see Table 4.2), where it showed the smallest drop in performance compared to the validation results.

It believes that the stability of the VisonLabs solution was caused by the diversity of networks in the final ensemble in terms of network architectures, pre-training tasks, and random seeds.

Qualitative Results

In this section, VisionLabs analyzes difficult examples by their proposed method. It runs four networks (namely A, B, C, and D in Table 4.1) on the Chalearn LAP challenge validation set and select examples with highest standard deviation (STD) on the liveness score among all samples. High STD implies conflicting predictions by different models. Figure 4.1 shows examples for which the networks disagree at most. As can be seen, the model D (which achieves the lowest TPR among all four models) tends to understate the live-

Table 4.2: Shrinkage of TPR@FPR= $10e^{-4}$ score on validation and test sets of Chalearn LAP face anti-spoofing challenge

	Valid	Test
Ours	100.00	99.8739
Team 2	100.00	99.8282
Team 3	100.00	99.8052
Team 4	100.00	98.1441
Team 5	99.9665	93.1550
Team 6	100.00	87.2094
Team 7	99.9665	25.0601

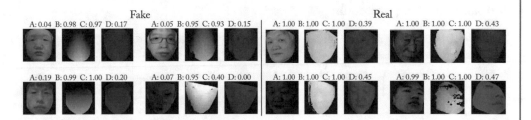

Figure 4.1: Examples of fake and real samples with highest standard deviation among predicted liveness scores from models A, B, C, and D. This figure is from Parkin and Grinchuk [2019].

ness score, assigning reals to fakes. But it is helpful in the case of hard fake examples, when two out of three other networks are wrong. Therefore, using only three models in the final ensemble would have led to lower score on the validation set.

Figure 4.2 demonstrates fakes and real samples which were close to the threshold at $FPR = 10e^4$. While they are distinguishable by human eye, one of the three modalities for every example looks similar to the normal one from the opposed class, so models based only on one modality may produce wrong predictions. Processing RGB, Depth, and IR channels together allows to overcome this issue.

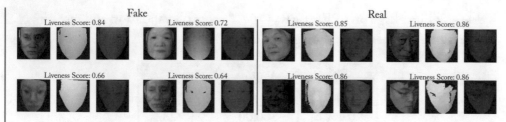

Figure 4.2: Examples of fake and real samples from validation subset where predicted liveness score is close to the threshold at $FPR = 10e^4$. This figure is from Parkin and Grinchuk [2019].

Table 4.3: The effect of modalities measured on the validation set. All models were pre-trained on the CASIA-Web face recognition task and fine tuned with the same learning protocol.

Modality	TPR@FPR=10^{-2}	TPR@FPR=10^{-3}	TPR@FPR=10^{-4}
RGB	71.74	22.34	7.85
IR	91.82	72.25	57.41
Depth	100.00	99.77	98.40
RGB+IR+Depth	100.00	100.00	99.87

Multi-Modality

Finally, VisionLabs examines the advantage of multi-modal networks over networks trained for each of the three modalities separately. It takes the proposed architecture with three branches and aggregation blocks, but instead of passing (RGB, IR, Depth) channels, it trained three models with (RGB, RGB, RGB), (IR, IR, IR) and (Depth, Depth, Depth) inputs. This allows a fair comparison with multi-modal network since all these architectures were identical and had the same number of parameters.

As can be seen from Table 4.3, using only RGB images results in low performance. The corresponding model overfitted to the training set and achieved only 7.85% TPR at $FPR = 10e^{-4}$. The IR-based model showed remarkably better results, reaching 57.41% TPR at $FPR = 10e^{-4}$ since IR images contained less identity details and the dataset size in this case was not so crucial as it was for the RGB model. The highest score of 98.40% TPR at $FPR = 10e^{-4}$ was achieved by the Depth modality, suggesting the importance of facial shape information for the anti-spoofing task.

However, the multi-modal network performed much better than the Depth network alone, reducing false rejection error from 1.6% to 0.13%, and showing the evidence of the synergetic effect of modality fusion.

4.1.2   2ND PLACE (TEAM NAME: READSENSE)

The overall architecture of ReadSense was shown in Section 3.2.2, where three branches (each branch per modality) and fusion strategy (namely, random modality feature learning). Readers can refer to Section 3.2.2 for the detailed information. Here, we only provide the experiment of ReadSense.

Implementation Details

The full-face images are resized to 112×112. ReadSense [Shen et al., 2019] uses random flipping, rotation, resizing, cropping for data augmentation. Patches are randomly extracted from the 112×112 full-face images. All models are trained on one Titan X(Pascal) GPU with a batch size of 512. It used the Stochastic Gradient Descent (SGD) optimizer with a cyclic cosine annealing learning rate schedule [Huang et al., 2017a]. The whole training procedure has 250 epochs and takes approximately 3 hours. Weight decay and momentum are set to 0.0005 and 0.9, respectively. It used PyTorch to training the network.

Results

To evaluate the effectiveness of the proposed model, ReadSense does several experiments with different configurations on the CASIA-SURF dataset. The details of comparison experiments are presented as below.

The Effect of Patch Sizes and Modality. In this setting, ReadSense uses different patch sizes using the same architecture in Fig. 3.3, i.e., 16×16, 32×32, 48×48 and 64×64. For fair comparisons, all the models are inferred 36 times with 9 non-overlapping image patches and 4 flipped input. As depicted in Table 4.4, for single modal input, among the three modalities, the depth data achieve the best performance of 0.8% (ACER), $TPR = 99.3\% @FPR = 10e^{-4}$. Specifically, fusing all the three modalities has strong performance across all patch sizes. It can be concluded that the proposed method by Readsense with fusion modality achieves the best results.

Table 4.4: The comparisons on different patch sizes and modalites. All models are trained on the CASIA-SURF training set and tested on the validation set.

Patch Size	Modal	ACER	TPR@FPR=10E^{-4}
16*16	RGB	4.5	94.9
	Depth	2.0	98.0
	IR	1.9	96.2
	Fusion	1.5	98.4
32*32	RGB	4.2	95.8
	Depth	0.8	99.3
	IR	1.5	98.1
	Fusion	0.0	100.0
48*48	RGB	3.1	96.1
	Depth	0.2	99.8
	IR	1.2	98.6
	Fusion	0.1	99.9
96*96	RGB	13.8	81.2
	Depth	5.2	92.8
	IR	13.4	81.4
	Fusion	1.7	97.9
Fullface	RGB	15.9	78.6
	Depth	8.8	88.6
	IR	11.3	84.3
	Fusion	4.8	93.7

The Effect of Modal Feature Erasing and Training strategy. ReadSense investigates how the random modal feature erasing and training strategy affect model performance for face anti-spoofing. "w.o CLR" denotes that one uses conventional SGD training with a standard decaying learning rate schedule until convergence instead of using cyclic learning rate. "w.o MFE" denotes that random modal features erasing are not applied. As shown in Table 4.5, both the cyclic learning rate and random modal feature erasing strategy are critical for achieving a high performance. After training the fusion model, it erases features from one modal and then evaluate the performance. ReadSense evaluates the

Table 4.5: The comparison on different training strategy. All models are trained with 32×32 size image patches.

Modal	ACER	TPR@FPR=10E^{-4}
Fusion (w.o. CLR-MFE)	1.60	98.0
Fusion (w.o. MFE)	0.60	98.5
Fusion (w.o. CLR)	0.60	99.2
Fusion	0.00	100.0
Fusion (Erase RGB)	0.51	99.3
Fusion (Erase Depth)	0.49	99.4
Fusion (Erase IR)	0.84	99.3
Fusion	0.00	100.0

performance of the trained fusion model with single modal feature erasing. In Table 4.5, from the validation score, one can conclude that the complementarity among different modalities can be learned to obtain better results.

Comparing with other teams in ChaLearn Face Anti-spoofing challenge. The final submission in this challenge is an ensemble result which combined outputs of three models in different patch sizes (32×32, 48×48, and 64×64) and it ranked the second place in the end. ReadSense is the only team that did not use the full-face image as model input. The result of $FN = 1$ shows that the patch-based learning method can effectively prevent the model from misclassifying the real face into an attack one by comparing with other top-ranked teams. As shown in Table 4.6, the results of the top three teams are significantly better than other teams on testing set. Especially, the TPR@FPR$= 10e - 4$ values of the ReadSense team and VisionLabs are relatively close, whereas VisionLabs applied plentiful data from other tasks to pretrain the model, and ReadSense only used a one-stage and end-to-end training schedule. Consequently, it also confirms the superiority of our solution.

4.1.3   3RD PLACE (TEAM NAME: FEATHER)

Implementation Detail

Data Augmentation. There are some differences in the images acquired by different devices, even if the same device model is used. As shown in Fig. 4.3, the

Table 4.6: Test set results and rankings of the final stage teams in ChaLearn Face Anti-spoofing attack detection challenge, the best indicators are bold

Team Name	FP	FN	APCER(%)	BPCER(%)	ACER(%)	TPR(%) @FPR=10⁻²	TPR(%) @FPR=10⁻³	TPR(%) @FPR=10⁻⁴
VisionLabs	**3**	27	**0.0074**	0.1546	**0.0810**	99.9885	**99.9541**	**99.8739**
ReadSense	77	**1**	0.1912	**0.0057**	0.0985	**100.0000**	99.9472	99.8052
Feather	48	53	0.1192	0.1392	0.1292	99.9541	99.8396	98.1441
Hahahaha	55	214	0.1366	1.2257	0.6812	99.6849	98.5909	93.1550
MAC-adv-group	825	30	2.0495	0.1718	1.1107	99.5131	97.2505	89.5579

Algorithm 4.1 Data Augmentation Algorithm

1: $scaler \leftarrow$ a random value in range [1/8, 1/5]
2: $offset \leftarrow$ a random value in range [100, 200]
3: $OutImg \leftarrow 0$
4: **for** $y = 0 \rightarrow Height - 1$ **do**
5:     **for** $x = 0 \rightarrow Width - 1$ **do**
6:         **if** $InImg(y, x) > 20$ **then**
7:             $off \leftarrow offset$
8:         **else**
9:             $off \leftarrow 0$
10:         $OutImg(y, x) \leftarrow$ InImg(y,x) * scaler + off
11: **return** $OutImg$

---

upper line is the depth images of the CASIA-SURF data set. The depth difference of the face part is small. It is difficult for the eyes to distinguish whether the face has a contour depth. The second line is the depth images of the MMFD[1] dataset whose outline of the faces are clearly showed. In order to reduce the data difference caused by the device, the depth of the real face images is scaled in MMFD which can be seen in the third line of Fig. 4.3. The way of data augmentation is presented in Algorithm 4.1.

Training Strategy. Pytorch [Paszke et al., 2017] is used to implement the proposed networks. It initializes all convolutions and FC layers with normal weight distribution [He et al., 2015]. For optimization solver, Stochastic Gradient Descent (SGD) is adopted with both learning rate beginning at 0.001, and decaying 0.1 after every 60 epochs, and momentum setting to 0.9. The Focal Loss [Lin et al., 2017] is employed with $\alpha = 1$ and $\gamma = 3$.

Result Analysis

How useful is MMFD dataset? A comparative experiment is executed to show the validity and generalization ability of our data. As shown in Table 4.7, the ACER of FeatherNetB with MMFD depth data is better than that with CASIA-SURF [Zhang et al., 2019b], though only 15 subjects are collected.

---

[1]This dataset is collected by the Feather Team, which is consisted of 15 subjects with 15,415 real samples and 28,438 fake samples.

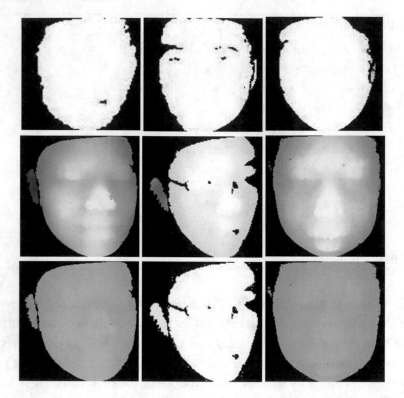

Figure 4.3: Depth image augmentation. (line 1): CAISA-SURF real depth images; (line 2): MMFD real depth images; and (line 3): our augmentation method on MMFD. This figure is from Zhang et al. [2019a].

Meanwhile, the experiment shows that the best option is to train the network with both data. The results of using the FeatherNetB are much better than the baselines that use multi-modal data fusion, indicating that the proposed network has better adaptability than the third-stream ResNet18 for baseline.

Compare with other network performance. As show in Table 4.8, experiments are executed to compare with other network's performance. All experimental results are based on depth of CASIA-SURF and MMFD depth images, and then the performance is verified on the CASIA-SURF verification set. It can be seen from Table 4.8 that the parameter size is much smaller, only 0.35M, while the performance on the verification set is the best.

Table 4.7: Performance of FeatherNetB training by different datasets. The third Column (from left to right) means the ACER value on the validation set of CASIA-SURF [Zhang et al., 2019b]. It shows that the generalization ability of MMFD is stronger than baseline of CASIA-SURF. The performance is better than the baseline method using multi-modal fusion.

Network	Training Dataset	ACER in Val
Baseline	CASIA-SURF	0.0213
FeatherNetB	CASIA-SURF depth	0.00971
FeatherNetB	MMFD depth	0.00677
FeatherNetB	CASIA-SURF + MMFD depth	**0.00168**

Table 4.8: Performance in validation dataset. Baseline is a way of fusing three modalities data (IR, RGB, Depth) through a three-stream network. Only depth data were used for training in the other networks. FeatherNetA and Feather-NetB have achieved higher performance with less parameters. Finally, the models are assembled to reduce ACER to 0.0.

Model	ACER	TPR @FPR=10^{-2}	TPR @FPR=10^{-3}	Params	FLOPS
ResNet18 [Zhang et al., 2019b]	0.05	0.883	0.272	11.18 M	1800 M
Baseline [Zhang et al., 2019b]	0.0213	0.9796	0.9469	–	–
FishNet150(our impl.)	0.00144	0.9996	0.998330	24.96 M	6452.72 M
MobilenetV2(1) (our impl.)	0.00228	0.9996	0.9993	2.23 M	306.17 M
ShuffleNetV2(1) (our impl.)	0.00451	1.0	0.98825	1.26 M	148.05
FeatherNetA	0.00261	1.0	0.961590	0.35 M	79.99 M
FeatherNetB	**0.00168**	**1.0**	**0.997662**	**0.35 M**	**83.05 M**

Table 4.9: Ablation experiments with different operations in CNNs

Model	FC	GAP	AP-down	ACER
Model 1	✗	✗	✗	0.00261
Model 2	✗	✗	✓	**0.00168**
Model 3	✓	✗	✗	0.00325
Model 4	✓	✓	✗	0.00525

Ablation Experiments. A number of ablations are executed to analyze different models with different layer combinations, shown in Table 4.9. The models are trained with CASIA-SURF training set and MMFD dataset.

Why AP-down in BlockB? Comparing *Model1 and Model2*, adding the Average Pooling branch to the secondary branch (called AP-down), as shown in block B of Fig. 3.6b, can effectively improve performance with a small number of parameters.

Why not use FC layer? Comparing *Model1 and Model3*, an FC layer doesn't reduce the error when adding a fully connected layer to the last layer of the network. Meanwhile, an FC layer is computationally expensive.

Why not use GAP layer? Comparing *Model3 and Model4*, it shows that adding global average pooling layer at the end of the network is not suitable for face anti-spoofing task. They will reduce performance.

Competition Details

The fusion procedure of FEATHER is applied in this competition. Meanwhile, the proposed FeatherNets with depth data only can provide a higher baseline alone (around 0.003 ACER). During the fusion procedure, the selected models are with different statistic features, and can help each other. For example, one model's characteristics of low False Negative (FN) are utilized to further eliminate the fake samples. The detailed procedure is described as below:

Training: The depth data are used to train seven models: FishNet150_1, FishNet150_2, MobilenetV2, FeatherNetA, FeatherNetB, FeatherNetBForIR, and ResNet_GC. Meanwhile, FishNet150_1, FishNet150_2 are models from

---

Algorithm 4.2 Ensemble Algorithm

1: $scores[] \leftarrow$

  score_FishNet150_1,

  score_FishNet150_2,

  score_ MobilenetV2,

  score_FeatherNetA,

  score_FeatherNetB,

  score_ResNet_GC

2: $mean\_score \leftarrow$ mean of scores[]

3: **if** $mean\_score > max\_threshold \ || \ mean\_score < min\_threshold$ **then**

4:      $final\_score \leftarrow mean\_score$

5: **else if** $score\_FishNet150\_1 < fish\_threshold$ **then**

6:      $final\_score \leftarrow score\_FishNet150\_1$

7: **else if** $score\_FeatherNetBForIR < IR\_threshold$ **then**

8:      $final\_score \leftarrow score\_FeatherNetBForIR$

9: **else**

10:      $mean\_score \leftarrow$

        (6 * mean_score + score_FishNet150_1) / 7

11:      **if** $mean\_score > 0.5$ **then**

12:          $final\_score \leftarrow$ max of scores[]

13:      **else**

14:          $final\_score \leftarrow$ min of scores[]

---

different epoch of FishNet. The IR data are used to train FeatherNetB as FeatherNetBforIR.

Inference: The inference scores will go through the "ensemble + cascade" process. The algorithm is shown as Algorithm 4.2.

Competition Result: The above procedure is used to get the result of 0.0013 (ACER), 0.999 (TPR@FPR= $10e-2$), 0.998 (TPR@FPR= $10e-3$) and 0.9814 (TPR@FPR= $10e-4$) in the test set and showed excellent performance in the Face Anti-spoofing challenge@CVPR2019.

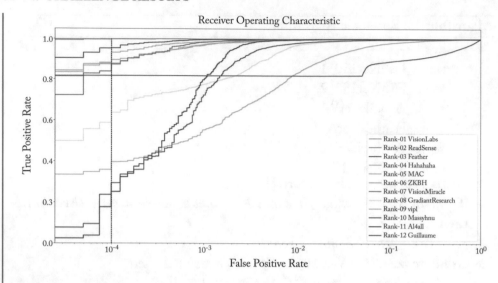

Figure 4.4: ROC curves of final stage teams on test set.

4.2   SUMMARY

4.2.1   CHALLENGE RESULTS REPORT

In order to evaluate the performance of solutions, it adopted the following metrics: APCER, NPCER, ACER, and TPR in the case of FPR= 10^{-2}, 10^{-3}, 10^{-4}, respectively, and the scores retained 6 decimal places for all results. The scores and ROC curves of participating teams on the testing partitions are shown in Table 4.10 and Fig. 4.4, respectively. Please note that although it reports performance for a variety of evaluation measures, the leading metric was TPR@FPR= 10^{-4}. One can be observed that the best result (VisionLabs) achieves TPR= 99.9885%, 99.9541%, 99.8739% @FPR= 10^{-2}, 10^{-3}, 10^{-4}, respectively, and the TP = 17430, FN = 28, FP = 1, TN = 40251, respectively on the test data set. In fact, different application scenarios have different requirements for each indicator, such as in higher security access control, the FP is required to be as small as possible, while a small FN value is more important in the case of troubleshoot suspects. Overall, the results of the first eight teams are better than the baseline method [Zhang et al., 2019b] when FPR = 10^{-4} on test data set.

Table 4.10: Results and rankings of the final stage teams on the test subset of CASIA-SURF, the best indicators are bold. Note that the results on the test set are tested by the model we trained according to the code submitted by the participating teams.

Team Name	FP	FN	APCER(%)	NPCER(%)	ACER(%)	TPR(%) @FPR=10^{-2}	TPR(%) @FPR=10^{-3}	TPR(%) @FPR=10^{-4}
VisionLabs	**3**	27	**0.0074**	0.1546	0.0810	99.9885	**99.9541**	**99.8739**
ReadSense	77	**1**	0.1912	**0.0057**	0.0985	**100.0000**	99.9472	99.8052
Feather	48	53	0.1192	0.1392	0.1292	99.9541	99.8396	98.1441
Hahahaha	55	214	0.1366	1.2257	0.6812	99.6849	98.5909	93.1550
MAC-adv-group	825	30	2.0495	0.1718	1.1107	99.5131	97.2505	89.5579
ZKBH	396	35	0.9838	0.2004	0.5921	99.7995	96.8094	87.6618
VisionMiracle	119	83	0.2956	0.4754	0.3855	99.9484	98.3274	87.2094
GradiantResearch	787	250	1.9551	1.4320	1.6873	97.0045	77.4302	63.5493
Baseline	1542	177	3.8308	1.0138	2.4223	96.7464	81.8321	56.8381
Vipl-bpoic	1580	985	3.9252	5.6421	4.7836	82.9877	55.1495	39.5520
Massyhnu	219	621	0.5440	3.5571	2.0505	98.0009	72.1961	29.2990
AI4all	273	100	0.6782	0.5728	0.6255	99.6334	79.7571	25.0601
Guillaume	5252	1869	13.0477	10.7056	11.8767	15.9530	1.5953	0.1595

Table 4.11: Provided by VisionLabs team. The results on the valid and test sets of the VisionLabs team, different NN modules represent different pre-trained Resnet [He et al., 2016].

NN1	NN1a	NN2	NN3	NN4	TPR @FPR=$10e^{-4}$(Val)	TPR @FPR=$10e^{-4}$(Test)
✓					0.9943	–
	✓				0.9987	–
		✓			0.9870	–
			✓		0.9963	–
				✓	0.9933	–
✓	✓				0.9963	–
✓	✓	✓			0.9983	–
✓		✓	✓		0.9997	–
✓		✓	✓	✓	1.0000	–
	✓	✓	✓	✓	**1.0000**	**0.9988**

4.2.2 CHALLENGE RESULTS ANALYSIS

As shown in Table 4.10, the results of the top three teams on test data set are clearly superior to other teams, revealing that ensemble learning has an exceptional advantage in deep learning compared to single model solutions under the same conditions, such as in Tables 4.11 and 4.4. Simultaneously, analyzing the stability of the results of all participating teams' submission from the ROC curve in Fig. 4.4, the three teams are significantly better than other teams on testing set (e.g., TPR@FPR= 10^{-4} values of these three teams are relatively close and superior to other teams). The team of ReadSense applies the image patch as input to emphasize the importance of local features in FAD task. The result of FN = 1 shows that the local feature can effectively prevent the model from misclassifying the real face into an attack one, shown in the blue box of Fig. 4.5.

Vipl-bpoic introduces the attention mechanism into FAD task. Different data modalities can provide different appearance information. The RGB data have rich details while the Depth data are sensitive to the distance between the image plane and the corresponding face. The IR data measure the amount of

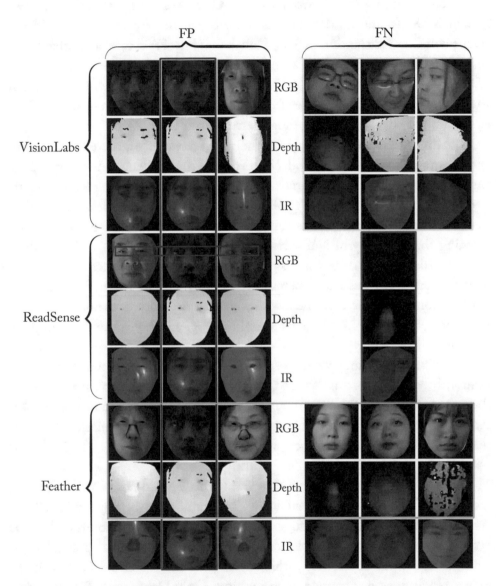

Figure 4.5: Mistaken samples of the top three teams on the testing data set, including FP and FN. Note that the models were trained by us. This figure is also from our workshop paper [Liu et al., 2019].

heat radiated from a face. Based on this characteristic, Feather uses a cascaded architecture with two subnetworks to study CASIA-SURF with two modalities, in which Depth and IR data are learned subsequently by each network. Some teams consider face landmark (e.g., Hahahaha) into FAD task, and other teams (e.g., MAC-adv-group, Massyhnu) focus on the color space conversion. Instead of binary classification model, ZKBH constructs a regression model to supervise the model to learn effective cues. GradiantResearch reformulates the face-PAD as an anomaly detection using deep metric learning.

Although these methods have their own advantages, there are still some shortcomings in the code reproduction stage of the challenge. As described before, CASIA-SURF is characterized by multi-modal data (i.e., RGB, Depth, and IR) and the main research point is how to fuse the complementary information between these three modalities. However, many teams apply ensemble learning that is a way of Naive Halfway Fusion [Zhang et al., 2019b], which cannot make full use of the characteristics between different modalities. In addition, most of the ensemble methods use greedy manner for model fusion, including constantly increase the model if the performance does not decrease on the valid set in Table 4.11, which inevitably brings additional time consumption and instability.

In order to demonstrate the shortcomings of the algorithm visually, we randomly selected six misclassified samples for each of the top three teams on the test set, of which the FP and FN are three respectively, as shown in Fig. 4.5. Notably, the fake sample in the red box was simultaneously misclassified into real face by the top three winners, where the clues were visually seen in the eye portion of the color modality.

From the misclassification samples of the VisionLabs team in Fig. 4.5, face pose is the main factor leading to FN samples (marked by a yellow box). As for the FP samples of ReadSense, the main clues are concentrated in the eye region (shown in the purple box). However, image patches applied by this team as the input of network, which is easy to cause misclassification if the image block does not contain an eye region. Only Depth and IR modal data sets were used by Feather team, resulting in misclassified samples that can be recognized by the human eyes easily. As shown in the green box, obvious clues which attached on the nose and eyes region in the color modal data sets are discarded by their algorithm.

On overall analysis, the top three teams have better recognition performance than Attack 1, 3, 5 for Attack 2, 4, 6 (performing a bending operation on the corresponding former) [Zhang et al., 2019b]. Figure 4.5 shows that the bending operation used by simulating the depth information of the real face is easily detected by the algorithms. Last but still notable, from the FP samples of the three teams, the misclassified samples are mainly caused by Attack 1, indicating that the sample with some regions are cut from the printed face can bring the depth information of the real face, but introducing more cues which can prove it is fake one.

C H A P T E R   5

Conclusions and Future Works

5.1   CONCLUSIONS

Recent advances in deep learning and biometric security, especially for face recognition systems, motivated us to focus on face anti-spoofing to explore the latest trends and go beyond traditional methods in computer vision and machine learning. For this reason, we organized the Chalearn Look at People Face Anti-spoofing Attack Workshop and Challenge at CVPR 2019.

We first presented the motivations and background of current face anti-spoofing research, and pointed out the drawbacks of limited data which would hinder the novel technology developments. Therefore, the largest dataset, namely CASIA-SURF, is released for face anti-spoofing. Then, based on this dataset, we organized a multi-modal face anti-spoofing challenge. This challenge attracted more than 300 teams, and the top-ranked participants in this challenge nearly obtained perfect performance. Finally, we gave a comprehensive review of multi-modal face anti-spoofing techniques, especially participants' methods.

5.2   FUTURE WORK

Besides the data size increase, there are several avenues that can be explored.

- The issue of ethnic bias has proven to affect the performance of face recognition in previous works, while it still remains to be absent in face anti-spoofing. A future work can explore the effectiveness of cross-ethnicity face presentation attack detection.

- 3D attacks are rarely considered as only limited data is released in current face anti-spoofing research. Diverse and large-scale datasets are welcome, such as different ethnicities, larger subjects, and diversity 2D and 3D attack types, such as print photo, video-replay, 3D print, and silica gel.

- The recent techniques that generate photo-realistic, fully synthetic "fake" facial images (such as deepfake, fakeswap) can be difficult to distinguish from the real ones. That would raise serious concerns about the trustworthiness of information in real life. Therefore, it is important to devise automatic and reliable methods that detect such types of manipulations.

For more information on face anti-spoofing recognition, please visit our office website: https://sites.google.com/qq.com/face-anti-spoofing/welcome.

Bibliography

Agarwal, A., Yadav, D., Kohli, N., Singh, R., Vatsa, M., and Noore, A. (2017). Face presentation attack with latex masks in multispectral videos. *CVPRW*, pp. 81–89. DOI: 10.1109/cvprw.2017.40. 4

Arashloo, S. R., Kittler, J., and Christmas, W. (2017). An anomaly detection approach to face spoofing detection: A new formulation and evaluation protocol. *IEEE Access*, 5:13,868–13,882. DOI: 10.1109/access.2017.2729161. 2

Atoum, Y., Liu, Y., Jourabloo, A., and Liu, X. (2017). Face anti-spoofing using patch and depth-based CNNs. *IEEE International Joint Conference on Biometrics (IJCB)*, pp. 319–328. DOI: 10.1109/btas.2017.8272713. 2, 7

Bharadwaj, S., Dhamecha, T. I., Vatsa, M., and Singh, R. (2013). Computationally efficient face spoofing detection with motion magnification. *Proc. of the IEEE Conference on Computer Vision and Pattern Recognition Workshops*, pp. 105–110. DOI: 10.1109/cvprw.2013.23. 6

Bhattacharjee, S., Mohammadi, A., and Marcel, S. (2018). Spoofing deep face recognition with custom silicone masks. *IEEE 9th International Conference on Biometrics Theory, Applications and Systems (BTAS)*, pp. 1–7. DOI: 10.1109/btas.2018.8698550. 1, 5

Boulkenafet, Z., Komulainen, J., and Hadid, A. (2016). Face spoofing detection using colour texture analysis. *IEEE Transactions on Information Forensics and Security*, 11(8):1818–1830. DOI: 10.1109/tifs.2016.2555286. 6

Boulkenafet, Z., Komulainen, J., and Hadid, A. (2017a). Face antispoofing using speeded-up robust features and fisher vector encoding. *IEEE Signal Processing Letters*, 24(2):141–145. DOI: 10.1109/lsp.2016.2630740. 1, 6

Boulkenafet, Z., Komulainen, J., Li, L., Feng, X., and Hadid, A. (2017b). OULU-NPU: A mobile face presentation attack database with real-world variations. *12th IEEE International Conference on Automatic Face and Gesture Recognition (FG)*, pp. 612–618. DOI: 10.1109/fg.2017.77. 4, 5

Chen, S., Liu, Y., Gao, X., and Han, Z. (2018). MobileFaceNets: Efficient CNNs for accurate real-time face verification on mobile devices. *Chinese Conference on Biometric Recognition*, pp. 428–438, Springer. DOI: 10.1007/978-3-319-97909-0_46. 26

Chingovska, I., Anjos, A., and Marcel, S. (2012a). On the effectiveness of local binary patterns in face anti-spoofing. *BIOSIG-Proc. of the International Conference of Biometrics Special Interest Group (BIOSIG)*, pp. 1–7, IEEE. 4, 5

Chingovska, I., Anjos, A., and Marcel, S. (2012b). On the effectiveness of local binary patterns in face anti-spoofing. *BIOSIG-Proc. of the International Conference of Biometrics Special Interest Group (BIOSIG)*, pp. 1–7, IEEE. 6

Chingovska, I., Erdogmus, N., Anjos, A., and Marcel, S. (2016). Face recognition systems under spoofing attacks. *Face Recognition Across the Imaging Spectrum*, pp. 165–194, Springer. DOI: 10.1007/978-3-319-28501-6_8. 1, 2, 4, 5

Chollet, F. (2017). Xception: Deep learning with depthwise separable convolutions. *Proc. of the IEEE Conference on Computer Vision and Pattern Recognition*, pp. 1251–1258. DOI: 10.1109/cvpr.2017.195. 27

Costa-Pazo, A., Bhattacharjee, S., Vazquez-Fernandez, E., and Marcel, S. (2016). The replay-mobile face presentation-attack database. *International Conference of the Biometrics Special Interest Group (BIOSIG)*, pp. 1–7, IEEE. DOI: 10.1109/biosig.2016.7736936. 4, 5

Costa-Pazo, A., Jiménez-Cabello, D., Vazquez-Fernandez, E., Alba-Castro, J. L., and López-Sastre, R. J. (2019). Generalized presentation attack detection: A face anti-spoofing evaluation proposal. *International Conference on Biometrics*. DOI: 10.1109/icb45273.2019.8987290. 32

De Marsico, M., Nappi, M., Riccio, D., and Dugelay, J. L. (2012). Moving face spoofing detection via 3D projective invariants. *International Conference on Biometrics (ICB)*, pp. 73–78, IEEE. DOI: 10.1109/icb.2012.6199761. 6

Deng, J., Dong, W., Socher, R., Li, L. J., Li, K., and Fei-Fei, L. (2009). ImageNet: A large-scale hierarchical image database. *IEEE Conference on Computer Vision and Pattern Recognition*, pp. 248–255. DOI: 10.1109/cvpr.2009.5206848. 2, 21, 31

Deng, J., Guo, J., Xue, N., and Zafeiriou, S. (2019). ArcFace: Additive angular margin loss for deep face recognition. *Proc. of the IEEE Conference on Computer Vision and Pattern Recognition*, pp. 4690–4699. DOI: 10.1109/cvpr.2019.00482. 26

Dhamecha, T. I., Singh, R., Vatsa, M., and Kumar, A. (2014). Recognizing disguised faces: Human and machine evaluation. *Plos One*, 9. DOI: 10.1371/journal.pone.0099212. 4

Duong, C. N., Quach, K. G., Le, N., Nguyen, N., and Luu, K. (2018). MobiFace: A lightweight deep learning face recognition on mobile devices. *ArXiv Preprint ArXiv:181111080.* 29

Erdogmus, N. and Marcel, S. (2014). Spoofing in 2D face recognition with 3D masks and anti-spoofing with kinect. *IEEE 9th International Conference on Biometrics Theory, Applications and Systems (BTAS)*, pp. 1–6. DOI: 10.1109/btas.2013.6712688. 3, 4, 5

Fatemifar, S., Arashloo, S. R., Awais, M., and Kittler, J. (2019a). Spoofing attack detection by anomaly detection. *ICASSP IEEE International Conference on Acoustics, Speech and Signal Processing (ICASSP)*, pp. 8464–8468. DOI: 10.1109/icassp.2019.8682253. 2

Fatemifar, S., Awais, M., Arashloo, S. R., and Kittler, J. (2019b). Combining multiple one-class classifiers for anomaly based face spoofing attack detection. *International Conference on Biometrics (ICB)*, pp. 1–7, IEEE. DOI: 10.1109/icb45273.2019.8987326. 2

Feng, L., Po, L. M., Li, Y., Xu, X., Yuan, F., Cheung, T. C. H., and Cheung, K. W. (2016). Integration of image quality and motion cues for face anti-spoofing: A neural network approach. *Journal of Visual Communication and Image Representation*, 38:451–460. DOI: 10.1016/j.jvcir.2016.03.019. 7

Feng, Y., Wu, F., Shao, X., Wang, Y., and Zhou, X. (2018). Joint 3D face reconstruction and dense alignment with position map regression network. *Proc. of the European Conference on Computer Vision (ECCV)*, pp. 534–551. DOI: 10.1007/978-3-030-01264-9_33. 11

de Freitas Pereira, T., Anjos, A., De Martino, J. M., and Marcel, S. (2013). Can face anti-spoofing countermeasures work in a real world scenario? *International Conference on Biometrics (ICB)*, pp. 1–8, IEEE. DOI: 10.1109/icb.2013.6612981. 1, 6

George, A., Mostaani, Z., Geissenbuhler, D., Nikisins, O., Anjos, A., and Marcel, S. (2019). Biometric face presentation attack detection with multi-channel convolutional neural network. *TIFS*. DOI: 10.1109/tifs.2019.2916652. 4

Guo, Y., Zhang, L., Hu, Y., He, X., and Gao, J. (2016). Ms-celeb-1m: Challenge of recognizing one million celebrities in the real world. *Electronic Imaging*, 11:1–6. DOI: 10.2352/issn.2470-1173.2016.11.imawm-463. 22, 40

He, K., Zhang, X., Ren, S., and Sun, J. (2015). Delving deep into rectifiers: Surpassing human-level performance on ImageNet classification. *Proc. of the IEEE International Conference on Computer Vision*, pp. 1026–1034. DOI: 10.1109/iccv.2015.123. 47

He, K., Zhang, X., Ren, S., and Sun, J. (2016). Deep residual learning for image recognition. *Proc. of the IEEE Conference on Computer Vision and Pattern Recognition*, pp. 770–778. DOI: 10.1109/cvpr.2016.90. 19, 26, 32, 33, 34, 54

Hernandez-Ortega, J., Fierrez, J., Morales, A., and Tome, P. (2018). Time analysis of pulse-based face anti-spoofing in visible and NIR. *Proc. of the IEEE Conference on Computer Vision and Pattern Recognition Workshops*, pp. 544–552. DOI: 10.1109/cvprw.2018.00096. 26

Holger, S., Sebastian, S., Andreas, K., and Norbert, J. (2016). Design of an active multispectral SWIR camera system for skin detection and face verification. *Journal of Sensors*, pp. 1–16. DOI: 10.1155/2016/9682453. 4

Howard, A. G., Zhu, M., Chen, B., Kalenichenko, D., Wang, W., Weyand, T., Andreetto, M., and Adam, H. (2017). MobileNets: Efficient convolutional neural networks for mobile vision applications. *ArXiv Preprint ArXiv:170404861.* 27

Hu, J., Shen, L., and Sun, G. (2018a). Squeeze-and-excitation networks. *Proc. of the IEEE Conference on Computer Vision and Pattern Recognition*. DOI: 10.1109/cvpr.2018.00745. 20

Hu, J., Shen, L., and Sun, G. (2018b). Squeeze-and-excitation networks. *Proc. of the IEEE Conference on Computer Vision and Pattern Recognition*, pp. 7132–7141. DOI: 10.1109/cvpr.2018.00745. 29, 30

Huang, G., Li, Y., Pleiss, G., Liu, Z., Hopcroft, J. E., and Weinberger, K. Q. (2017a). Snapshot ensembles: Train 1, get *m* for free. *ArXiv Preprint ArXiv:170400109.* 43

Huang, G., Liu, Z., Van Der Maaten, L., and Weinberger, K. Q. (2017b). Densely connected convolutional networks. *Proc. of the IEEE Conference on Computer Vision and Pattern Recognition*, pp. 4700–4708. 26

Jourabloo, A., Liu, Y., and Liu, X. (2018). Face de-spoofing: Anti-spoofing via noise modeling. *Proc. of the European Conference on Computer Vision (ECCV)*, pp. 290–306. DOI: 10.1007/978-3-030-01261-8_18. 2, 7

Kim, S., Yu, S., Kim, K., Ban, Y., and Lee, S. (2013). Face liveness detection using variable focusing. *International Conference on Biometrics (ICB)*, pp. 1–6, IEEE. DOI: 10.1109/icb.2013.6613002. 6

Kim, Y., Na, J., Yoon, S., and Yi, J. (2009). Masked fake face detection using radiance measurements. *JOSA A*, 26(4):760–766. DOI: 10.1364/josaa.26.000760. 5

King, D. E. (2009). Dlib-ml: A machine learning toolkit. *JMLR*, 10:1755–1758. 11

Kollreider, K., Fronthaler, H., and Bigun, J. (2008). Verifying liveness by multiple experts in face biometrics. *IEEE Computer Society Conference on Computer Vision and Pattern Recognition Workshops*, pp. 1–6. DOI: 10.1109/cvprw.2008.4563115. 6

Komulainen, J., Hadid, A., and Pietikäinen, M. (2013a). Context based face anti-spoofing. *IEEE 6th International Conference on Biometrics: Theory, Applications and Systems (BTAS)*, pp. 1–8. DOI: 10.1109/btas.2013.6712690. 1

Komulainen,, J., Hadid, A., and Pietikäinen, M. (2013b). Context based face anti-spoofing. *IEEE 6th International Conference on Biometrics: Theory, Applications and Systems (BTAS)*, pp. 1–8. DOI: 10.1109/btas.2013.6712690. 6

Komulainen, J., Hadid, A., Pietikäinen, M., Anjos, A., and Marcel, S. (2013c). Complementary countermeasures for detecting scenic face spoofing attacks. *International Conference on Biometrics (ICB)*, pp. 1–7, IEEE. DOI: 10.1109/icb.2013.6612968. 6

Kose, N. and Dugelay, J. L. (2013). Countermeasure for the protection of face recognition systems against mask attacks. *10th IEEE International Conference and Workshops on Automatic Face and Gesture Recognition (FG)*, pp. 1–6. DOI: 10.1109/fg.2013.6553761. 5

Li, J., Wang, Y., Tan, T., and Jain, A. K. (2004). Live face detection based on the analysis of Fourier spectra. *Biometric Technology for Human Identification*, 5404:296–304, International Society for Optics and Photonics. DOI: 10.1117/12.541955. 6

Li, L., Feng, X., Boulkenafet, Z., Xia, Z., Li, M., and Hadid, A. (2016). An original face anti-spoofing approach using partial convolutional neural network. *6th International Conference on Image Processing Theory, Tools and Applications (IPTA)*, pp. 1–6, IEEE. DOI: 10.1109/ipta.2016.7821013. 7, 26

Lin, M., Chen, Q., and Yan, S. (2013). Network in network. *ArXiv Preprint ArXiv:13124400.* 26

Lin, T. Y., Goyal, P., Girshick, R., He, K., and Dollár, P. (2017). Focal loss for dense object detection. *Proc. of the IEEE International Conference on Computer Vision*, pp. 2980–2988. DOI: 10.1109/iccv.2017.324. 47

Liu, A., Wan, J., Escalera, S., Jair Escalante, H., Tan, Z., Yuan, Q., Wang, K., Lin, C., Guo, G., Guyon, I., et al. (2019). Multi-modal face anti-spoofing attack detection challenge at CVPR. *Proc. of the IEEE Conference on Computer Vision and Pattern Recognition Workshops*. DOI: 10.1109/cvprw.2019.00202. 55

Liu, S., Yang, B., Yuen, P. C., and Zhao, G. (2016). A 3D mask face anti-spoofing database with real world variations. *CVPRW*, pp. 100–106. DOI: 10.1109/cvprw.2016.193. 4

Liu, Y., Jourabloo, A., and Liu, X. (2018). Learning deep models for face anti-spoofing: Binary or auxiliary supervision. *Proc. of the IEEE Con-*

ference on Computer Vision and Pattern Recognition, pp. 389–398. DOI: 10.1109/cvpr.2018.00048. 2, 4, 5, 7, 14

Liu, Y., Stehouwer, J., Jourabloo, A., and Liu, X. (2019b). Deep tree learning for zero-shot face anti-spoofing. *Proc. of the IEEE Conference on Computer Vision and Pattern Recognition*, pp. 4680–4689. DOI: 10.1109/cvpr.2019.00481. 4

Long, J. L., Zhang, N., and Darrell, T. (2014). Do ConvNets learn correspondence? *Advances in Neural Information Processing Systems*, pp. 1601–1609. 26

Luo, W., Li, Y., Urtasun, R., and Zemel, R. (2016). Understanding the effective receptive field in deep convolutional neural networks. *Advances in Neural Information Processing Systems*, pp. 4898–4906. 26

Ma, N., Zhang, X., Zheng, H. T., and Sun, J. (2018). ShuffleNet v2: Practical guidelines for efficient CNN architecture design. *Proc. of the European Conference on Computer Vision (ECCV)*, pp. 116–131. DOI: 10.1007/978-3-030-01264-9_8. 26, 29, 32

Maatta, J., Hadid, A., and Pietikainen, M. (2012). Face spoofing detection from single images using texture and local shape analysis. *IET Biometrics*, 1(1):3–10. DOI: 10.1049/iet-bmt.2011.0009. 6

Manjani, I., Tariyal, S., Vatsa, M., Singh, R., and Majumdar, A. (2017). Detecting silicone maskbased presentation attack via deep dictionary learning. *TIFS*, 12(7):1713–1723. DOI: 10.1109/tifs.2017.2676720. 4

Nikisins, O., Mohammadi, A., Anjos, A., and Marcel, S. (2018). On effectiveness of anomaly detection approaches against unseen presentation attacks in face anti-spoofing. *International Conference on Biometrics (ICB)*, pp. 75–81, IEEE. DOI: 10.1109/icb2018.2018.00022. 2

Niu, Z., Zhou, M., Wang, L., Gao, X., and Hua, G. (2016). Ordinal regression with multiple output CNN for age estimation. *Proc. of the IEEE Conference on Computer Vision and Pattern Recognition*, pp. 4920–4928. DOI: 10.1109/cvpr.2016.532. 22, 40

Ojala, T., Pietikäinen, M., and Mäenpää, T. (2002). Multiresolution gray-scale and rotation invariant texture classification with local binary patterns. *IEEE Transactions on Pattern Analysis and Machine Intelligence*, (7):971–987. DOI: 10.1109/tpami.2002.1017623. 6

Pan, G., Sun, L., Wu, Z., and Lao, S. (2007). Eyeblink-based anti-spoofing in face recognition from a generic webcamera. *IEEE 11th International Conference on Computer Vision*, pp. 1–8. DOI: 10.1109/iccv.2007.4409068. 6

Pan, G., Sun, L., Wu, Z., and Wang, Y. (2011). Monocular camera-based face liveness detection by combining eyeblink and scene context. *Telecommunication Systems*, 47(3–4):215–225. DOI: 10.1007/s11235-010-9313-3. 6

Parkin, A. and Grinchuk, O. (2019). Recognizing multi-modal face spoofing with face recognition networks. *The IEEE Conference on Computer Vision and Pattern Recognition (CVPR) Workshops*. DOI: 10.1109/cvprw.2019.00204. 21, 22, 23, 37, 38, 39, 41, 42

Paszke, A., Gross, S., Chintala, S., Chanan, G., Yang, E., DeVito, Z., Lin, Z., Desmaison, A., Antiga, L., and Lerer, A. (2017). Automatic differentiation in pytorch. 37, 47

Patel, K., Han, H., and Jain, A. K. (2016a). Cross-database face antispoofing with robust feature representation. *Chinese Conference on Biometric Recognition*, pp. 611–619, Springer. DOI: 10.1007/978-3-319-46654-5_67. 26

Patel, K., Han, H., and Jain, A. K. (2016b). Secure face unlock: Spoof detection on smartphones. *IEEE Transactions on Information Forensics and Security*, 11(10):2268–2283. DOI: 10.1109/tifs.2016.2578288. 1, 3, 6, 7

Peng, F., Qin, L., and Long, M. (2018a). Ccolbp: Chromatic co-occurrence of local binary pattern for face presentation attack detection. *27th International Conference on Computer Communication and Networks (ICCCN)*, pp. 1–9, IEEE. DOI: 10.1109/icccn.2018.8487325. 33

Peng, F., Qin, L., and Long, M. (2018b). Face presentation attack detection using guided scale texture. *Multimedia Tools and Applications*, pp. 1–27. DOI: 10.1007/s11042-017-4780-0. 33

Qin, Z., Zhang, Z., Chen, X., Wang, C., and Peng, Y. (2018). FD-mobileNet: Improved mobileNet with a fast downsampling strategy. *25th IEEE International Conference on Image Processing (ICIP)*, pp. 1363–1367. DOI: 10.1109/icip.2018.8451355. 29

Raghavendra, R., Raja, K. B., and Busch, C. (2015). Presentation attack detection for face recognition using light field camera. *TIP*. DOI: 10.1109/tip.2015.2395951. 4

Raghavendra, R., Raja, K. B., Venkatesh, S., Cheikh, F. A., and Busch, C. (2017). On the vulnerability of extended multispectral face recognition systems towards presentation attacks. *ISBA*, pp. 1–8. DOI: 10.1109/isba.2017.7947698. 4

Sandler, M., Howard, A., Zhu, M., Zhmoginov, A., and Chen, L. C. (2018). MobileNetV2: Inverted residuals and linear bottlenecks. *Proc. of the IEEE Conference on Computer Vision and Pattern Recognition*, pp. 4510–4520. DOI: 10.1109/cvpr.2018.00474. 26, 28

Schwartz, W. R., Rocha, A., and Pedrini, H. (2011). Face spoofing detection through partial least squares and low-level descriptors. *International Joint Conference on Biometrics (IJCB)*, pp. 1–8, IEEE. DOI: 10.1109/ijcb.2011.6117592. 6

Shao, R., Lan, X., Li, J., and Yuen, P. C. (2019). Multi-adversarial discriminative deep domain generalization for face presentation attack detection. *Proc. of the IEEE Conference on Computer Vision and Pattern Recognition*, pp. 10,023–10,031. DOI: 10.1109/cvpr.2019.01026. 2, 7

Shen, T., Huang, Y., and Tong, Z. (2019). FaceBagNet: Bag-of-local-features model for multi-modal face anti-spoofing. *Proc. of the IEEE Conference on Computer Vision and Pattern Recognition Workshops*. DOI: 10.1109/cvprw.2019.00203. 21, 23, 24, 25, 26, 37, 43

Simonyan, K. and Zisserman, A. (2014). Very deep convolutional networks for large-scale image recognition. *ArXiv Preprint ArXiv:14091556*. 33, 34

Sun, K., Li, M., Liu, D., and Wang, J. (2018). IGVC3: Interleaved low-rank group convolutions for efficient deep neural networks. *ArXiv Preprint ArXiv:180600178*. 26

Szegedy, C., Liu, W., Jia, Y., Sermanet, P., Reed, S., Anguelov, D., Erhan, D., Vanhoucke, V., and Rabinovich, A. (2015). Going deeper with convolutions. *Proc. of the IEEE Conference on Computer Vision and Pattern Recognition*, pp. 1–9. DOI: 10.1109/cvpr.2015.7298594. 28

Tan, X., Li, Y., Liu, J., and Jiang, L. (2010). Face liveness detection from a single image with sparse low rank bilinear discriminative model. *European Conference on Computer Vision*, pp. 504–517, Springer. DOI: 10.1007/978-3-642-15567-3_37. 6

Tronci, R., Muntoni, D., Fadda, G., Pili, M., Sirena, N., Murgia, G., Ristori, M., Ricerche, S., and Roli, F. (2011). Fusion of multiple clues for photo-attack detection in face recognition systems. *International Joint Conference on Biometrics (IJCB)*, pp. 1–6, IEEE. DOI: 10.1109/ijcb.2011.6117522. 6

Wang, L., Ding, X., and Fang, C. (2009). Face live detection method based on physiological motion analysis. *Tsinghua Science and Technology*, 14(6):685–690. DOI: 10.1016/s1007-0214(09)70135-x. 6

Wang, T., Yang, J., Lei, Z., Liao, S., and Li, S. Z. (2013). Face liveness detection using 3D structure recovered from a single camera. *International Conference on Biometrics (ICB)*, pp. 1–6, IEEE. DOI: 10.1109/icb.2013.6612957. 6

Wang, Z., Zhao, C., Qin, Y., Zhou, Q., and Lei, Z. (2018). Exploiting temporal and depth information for multi-frame face anti-spoofing. *ArXiv Preprint ArXiv:181105118*. 26

Wang, Z., Yu, Z., Zhao, C., Zhu, X., Qin, Y., Zhou, Q., Zhou, F., and Lei, Z. (2020). Deep spatial gradient and temporal depth learning for face anti-spoofing. *Proc. of the IEEE/CVF Conference on Computer Vision and Pattern Recognition*, pp. 5042–5051. 7

Wen, D., Han, H., and Jain, A. K. (2015). Face spoof detection with image distortion analysis. *IEEE Transactions on Information Forensics and Security*, 10(4):746–761. DOI: 10.1109/tifs.2015.2400395. 4, 5

Wen, Y., Zhang, K., Li, Z., and Qiao, Y. (2016). A discriminative feature learning approach for deep face recognition. *European Conference on Computer Vision*, pp. 499–515, Springer. DOI: 10.1007/978-3-319-46478-7_31. 33

Wu, B., Wan, A., Yue, X., Jin, P., Zhao, S., Golmant, N., Gholaminejad, A., Gonzalez, J., and Keutzer, K. (2018a). Shift: A zero flop, zero parameter alternative to spatial convolutions. *Proc. of the IEEE Conference on Computer Vision and Pattern Recognition*, pp. 9127–9135. DOI: 10.1109/cvpr.2018.00951. 26

Wu, X., He, R., Sun, Z., and Tan, T. (2018b). A light CNN for deep face representation with noisy labels. *IEEE Transactions on Information Forensics and Security*, 13(11):2884–2896. DOI: 10.1109/tifs.2018.2833032. 33

Xie, J., He, T., Zhang, Z., Zhang, H., Zhang, Z., and Li, M. (2018). Bag of tricks for image classification with convolutional neural networks. *ArXiv Preprint ArXiv:181201187*. DOI: 10.1109/cvpr.2019.00065. 29

Xie, S., Girshick, R., Dollár, P., Tu, Z., and He, K. (2017). Aggregated residual transformations for deep neural networks. *Proc. of the IEEE Conference on Computer Vision and Pattern Recognition*, pp. 1492–1500. DOI: 10.1109/cvpr.2017.634. 24, 31

Yang, J., Lei, Z., Liao, S., and Li, S. Z. (2013). Face liveness detection with component dependent descriptor. *International Conference on Biometrics (ICB)*, pp. 1–6, IEEE. DOI: 10.1109/icb.2013.6612955. 1, 6

Yang, J., Lei, Z., and Li, S. Z. (2014). Learn convolutional neural network for face anti-spoofing. *ArXiv Preprint ArXiv:14085601*. 7

Yi, D., Lei, Z., Liao, S., and Li, S. Z. (2014). Learning face representation from scratch. *ArXiv Preprint ArXiv:14117923*. 1, 2, 22, 39, 40

Yu, Z., Zhao, C., Wang, Z., Qin, Y., Su, Z., Li, X., Zhou, F., and Zhao, G. (2020). Searching central difference convolutional networks for face anti-spoofing. *Proc. of the IEEE/CVF Conference on Computer Vision and Pattern Recognition*, pp. 5295–5305. 7

Zhang, P., Zou, F., Wu, Z., Dai, N., Mark, S., Fu, M., Zhao, J., and Li, K. (2019a). FeatherNets: Convolutional neural networks as light as feather for face anti-spoofing. *Proc. of the IEEE Conference on Computer Vision and Pattern Recognition Workshops*. DOI: 10.1109/cvprw.2019.00199. 21, 26, 27, 37, 48

Zhang, S., Wang, X., Liu, A., Zhao, C., Wan, J., Escalera, S., Shi, H., Wang, Z., and Li, S. Z. (2019b). A dataset and benchmark for large-scale multi-modal face anti-spoofing. *Proc. of the IEEE Conference on Computer Vision and Pattern Recognition*, pp. 919–928. DOI: 10.1109/cvpr.2019.00101. 2, 3, 4, 22, 25, 31, 38, 47, 49, 52, 56, 57

Zhang, S., Liu, A., Wan, J., Liang, Y., Guo, G., Escalera, S., Escalante, H. J., and Li, S. Z. (2020). Casia-Surf: A large-scale multi-modal benchmark for face anti-spoofing. *IEEE Transactions on Biometrics, Behavior, and Identity Science*, 2(2):182–193. DOI: 10.1109/tbiom.2020.2973001. 3

Zhang, Z., Yan, J., Liu, S., Lei, Z., Yi, D., and Li, S. Z. (2012). A face antispoofing database with diverse attacks. *IEEE*, pp. 26–31. DOI: 10.1109/icb.2012.6199754. 4, 5

Zhao, J., Cheng, Y., Xu, Y., Xiong, L., Li, J., Zhao, F., Jayashree, K., Pranata, S., Shen, S., Xing, J., et al. (2018). Towards pose invariant face recognition in the wild. *CVPR*, pp. 2207–2216. DOI: 10.1109/cvpr.2018.00235. 22, 40

Authors' Biographies

JUN WAN

Jun Wan received a B.S. degree from the China University of Geosciences, Beijing, China, in 2008, and a Ph.D. degree from the Institute of Information Science, Beijing Jiaotong University, Beijing, China, in 2015. Since January 2015, he has been a Faculty Member with the National Laboratory of Pattern Recognition (NLPR), Institute of Automation, Chinese Academy of Science (CASIA), China, where he currently serves as an Associate Professor. He is an IEEE Senior Member and a director of Chalearn Challenges. He has published more than 50 research papers and has been guest editor at *TPAMI*, *MVA*, and *Entropy*. His main research interests include computer vision, machine learning, especially for face and pedestrian analysis (such as attribute analysis, face anti-spoofing detection), gesture and sign language recognition. He has published papers in top journals and conferences, such as JMLR, T-PAMI, T-IP, T-MM, T-CYB, TOMM, PR, CVIU, CVPR, AAAI, and IJCAI. He has served as the reviewer on several journals and conferences, such as JMLR, T-PAMI, T-IP, T-MM, T-SMC, PR, CVPR, ICCV, ECCV, AAAI, and ICRA.

GUODONG GUO

Guodong Guo received a B.E. degree in automation from Tsinghua University, Beijing, China, and a Ph.D. degree in computer science from University of Wisconsin, Madison, WI. He is currently the Deputy Head of the Institute of Deep Learning, Baidu Research, and also an Associate Professor with the Department of Computer Science and Electrical Engineering, West Virginia University (WVU). In the past, he visited and worked in several places, including INRIA, Sophia Antipolis, France; Ritsumeikan University, Kyoto, Japan; and Microsoft Research, Beijing, China; He authored a book, *Face, Expression, and Iris Recognition Using Learning-based Approaches* (2008), co-edited two books, *Support Vector Machines Applications* (2014) and *Mobile Biometrics* (2017), and published over 100 technical papers. He is an Associate Editor of

IEEE Transactions on Affective Computing, Journal of Visual Communication and Image Representation, and serves on the editorial board of IET Biometrics. His research interests include computer vision, biometrics, machine learning, and multimedia.

He received the North Carolina State Award for Excellence in Innovation in 2008, Outstanding Researcher (2017–2018, 2013–2014) at CEMR, WVU, and New Researcher of the Year (2010–2011) at CEMR, WVU. He was selected the "People's Hero of the Week" by BSJB under Minority Media and Telecommunications Council (MMTC) in 2013. Two of his papers were selected as "The Best of FG'13" and "The Best of FG'15", respectively.

SERGIO ESCALERA

Sergio Escalera (www.sergioescalera.com) obtained a P.h.D. degree on multi-class visual categorization systems at Computer Vision Center, UAB. He obtained the 2008 best Thesis award on Computer Science at Universitat Autonoma de Barcelona. He is ICREA Academia. He leads the Human Pose Recovery and Behavior Analysis Group at UB, CVC, and the Barcelona Graduate School of Mathematics. He is Full Professor at the Department of Mathematics and Informatics, Universitat de Barcelona. He is an adjunct professor at Universitat Oberta de Catalunya, Aalborg University, and Dalhousie University. He has been visiting professor at TU Delft and Aalborg Universities. He is also a member of the Computer Vision Center at UAB. He is series editor of *The Springer Series on Challenges in Machine Learning.* He is a member and fellow of the European Laboratory of Intelligent Systems ELLIS. He is vice-president of ChaLearn Challenges in Machine Learning, leading ChaLearn Looking at People events. He is a co-creator of Codalab open source platform for challenges organization. He is Chair of IAPR TC-12: Multimedia and visual information systems. His research interests include: statistical pattern recognition, affective computing, and human pose recovery and behavior understanding, including multi-modal data analysis, with special interest in characterizing people: personality and psychological profile computing.

HUGO JAIR ESCALANTE

Hugo Jair Escalante received a Ph.D. degree in computer science, for which he received the best Ph.D. thesis on Artificial Intelligence 2010 award (Mexican Society in Artificial Intelligence). He is a researcher scientist at Instituto Nacional de Astrofisica, Optica y Electronica, INAOE, Mexico. In 2017, he received the UANL research award in exact sciences. He is secretary and member of the board of directors of ChaLearn, a non-profit organism dedicated to organizing challenges, since 2011. He is information officer of the IAPR Technical Committee 12. Since 2017, he is the editor of the Springer Series on Challenges in Machine Learning. He has been involved in the organization of several challenges in machine learning and computer vision, collocated with top venues; see http://chalearnlap.cvc.uab.es/. He has served as co-editor of special issues in the *International Journal of Computer Vision*, the *IEEE Transactions on Pattern Analysis and Machine Intelligence*, and the *IEEE Transactions on Affective Computing*. He has served as area chair for NIPS 2016–2018, he is data competition chair of PAKDD 2018, and has been member of the program committee of venues like CVPR, ICPR, ICCV, ECCV, ICML, NIPS, and IJCNN. His research interests are on machine learning, challenge organization, and its applications on language and vision.

STAN Z. LI

Stan Z. Li received a BEng degree from Hunan University, China, a MEng degree from National University of Defense Technology, China, and a Ph.D. degree from Surrey University, United Kingdom. He is currently a chair professor of Westlake University. Before that, he was a professor and the director of Center for Biometrics and Security Research (CBSR), Institute of Automation, Chinese Academy of Sciences (CASIA), and was at Microsoft Research Asia, as a researcher from 2000–2004. Prior to that, he was an associate professor at Nanyang Technological University, Singapore. His research interests include pattern recognition and machine learning, image and vision processing, face recognition, biometrics, and intelligent video surveillance. He has published more than 200 papers in international journals and conferences, and authored and edited 8 books. He was an associate editor of the *IEEE Transactions on Pattern Analysis and Machine Intelligence* and is acting as the editor-in-chief for the *Encyclopedia of Biometrics*. He served as a program cochair for the International Conference on Biometrics 2007 and 2009, and has been involved in organizing other international conferences and workshops in the fields of his research interest. He was elevated to IEEE fellow for his contributions to the fields of face recognition, pattern recognition, and computer vision, and he is a member of the IEEE Computer Society.

Printed in the United States
by Baker & Taylor Publisher Services